Contents

Subject 6 – Insurance – Page 72

Subject 7 – Construction & Use – Page 78

Subject 8 – Driver Licensing & Forgery Of Documents (Sergeants syllabus only) – Page 87

Subject 9 – Notice of Intended Prosecution (NIPs) (Sergeants syllabus only) – Page 97

Subject 10 – Fixed Penalty System (Sergeants syllabus only) – Page 101

Free 1 Day Revision Kick Start Courses

Register for a free 1 day crammer course at **www.policepass.co.uk**
During the course you will receive **several hours of free lectures** on key topics within the examination syllabus from our team of operational Detective Inspectors who have all **been there and done it** - **passing the Inspectors OSPRE Part 1 exam themselves in the top 1% nationally.**

Free Video Revision Guidance & Examination Statistics

Do you want to know the questions you will be asked when you sit the exam?

Log onto out website at **www.policepass.co.uk** for **free** downloads of **statistical guidance on examination trends** complied over several years.

You can also view a **free video seminar** by the Police Pass team offering you tips on the areas of the examination syllabus that the examiner will definitely test your knowledge of and more importantly how the examiner will seek to catch you out on the big day.

Authors

Adrian Williams
Solicitor

Adrian is a solicitor of the Supreme Court of England & Wales and is an accredited police station adviser. He over a decade's experience as a Senior University Law Lecturer, teaching criminal procedure and evidence at both undergraduate and postgraduate levels. He has an extensive research profile having published numerous articles in both national and international legal journals.

Inspector Greg Williams

Greg is an operational Detective Inspector with Dyfed-Powys police force. Greg passed the OSPRE Part 1 Inspectors examination in the top 0.5% of candidates in England &Wales and his paper was officially graded as "exceptional".

Eighth Edition - Blue Light Publishing Limited 2012 ©

The law is as stated at 1st September 2011.

ISBN: 978-0-9570020-0-5

Road Policing
Subject 1: Standards of Driving

A - Definitions

Definition Of A Mechanically Propelled Vehicle

A **mechanically propelled vehicle (MPV)** includes any vehicle powered by **either**:				
Petrol	Gas	Diesel	Electricity	Steam

Definition Of A Motor Vehicle – Section 185(1) Road Traffic Act 1988

A **motor vehicle** is defined as an **MPV** which is **either**:	
Intended	**Adapted**
...for use **on a road.**	

Exam Trip Up – What Is Not A Motor Vehicle?

Examples that are **not** motor vehicles include:		
Off road scrambler bikes.	Drag racers.	Fork lift trucks.

Exam Trip Up – What Is Neither An MPV Or A Motor Vehicle

- The Road Traffic Act 1988 expressly states that:
  - **Neither:**
    - **Electronically assisted pedal cycles;** or
    - **Invalid carriages;**
  - Are either:
    - **Motor vehicles;** or
    - **Mechanically propelled vehicles.**

Definition Of A Road – Section 192(1) Road Traffic Act 1988

The definition of a **road** includes **any**:		
Highway.	**Road** to which the **public have access.**	**Bridges** over which a **road passes.**

Definition Of A Highway

The definition of a **highway** includes **any**:		
Public footpaths.	**Public bridleways.**	**Public carriageways.**

Definition Of Driving

There is **no statutory definition** of driving - it is a **question of fact** - determined by whether the person had **control** of **both** the vehicle's:	
Movement.	**Direction.**

Exam Trip Up

- There must be **admissible evidence** of the aforementioned factors.
- A mere suspicion, no matter how strong will be insufficient to prove that driving had taken place.

Definition Of Dangerous: An Objective Test – Section 2A(1) Road Traffic Act 1988

Driving will be deemed to be **dangerous** where <u>both</u>:	
Step 1	**Step 2**
The person's driving **falls far below** the **standards** of a **competent** and **careful** driver....	...and it would be **obvious to a competent and careful driver** (objective test) that either: ■ **Driving that way** would be **dangerous;** or ■ **Driving** the vehicle in its **current state** would be **dangerous.**

What Must The Danger Relate To?

The **danger** must relate to <u>either</u>:	
Danger 1	**Danger 2**
Injury to any **person.**	**Serious damage** to **property.**

Current State Of The Vehicle

- **Current state** of the vehicle implies something **different** to its **original state.**
- For example – if a tractor was **manufactured** with a **spike** attached to its front the dangerous spike formed part of its **original state** – *R v Marchant and Muntz* [2003] Crim LR 806.

The State Of The Vehicle

Regard can be had for anything **either**:		
Factor 1	**Factor 2**	**Factor 3**
Attached to the vehicle.	**Carried in** or **on** the vehicle.	The **manner** in which it was **either**: ■ Carried; or ■ Attached.

Exam Trip Up

- Police drivers will be judged against the same standard of care as other drivers - *Wood v Richards* [1977] RTR 201.
- There is no special exemption for police drivers or any other emergency crews - *R v O'Toole* [1971] 55 Cr App R 206.
- The Court of Appeal in the case of *Keyse* v *Commissioner of the Metropolitan Police* [2001] EWHC Civ. 715, reviewed the issues of civil liability arising from police drivers and provided the following direction:

  '*police and other emergency service drivers were entitled to expect other road users to take note of the signs of their approach (e.g sirens & flashing lights) and where appropriate, react accordingly*'.

B - Dangerous Driving & Causing Death By Dangerous Driving

Dangerous Driving	Causing Death By Dangerous Driving
Section 2 Road Traffic Act 1988	**Section 1 Road Traffic Act 1988**
A person commits an offence of **dangerous driving** if they: ■ **Drive** an **MPV;** ☐ **Dangerously;** ☐ On either: ■ A **road;** or ■ Other **public place.**	A person commits an offence of **death by dangerous driving** if they: ☐ **Unlawfully;** ☐ **Cause** the **death;** ☐ Of another **human being;** ☐ By **driving** an **MPV;** ☐ **Dangerously;** ☐ On a: ■ **Road;** or ■ Other **public place.**
Either Way Offence Penalty In The Crown Court - Two Years Imprisonment And / Or A Fine Penalty In The Magistrates Court - Six Months Imprisonment And / Or A Fine Plus Obligatory Disqualification & Compulsory Re-Testing	Indictable Only Offence Penalty In The Crown Court - 14 Years Imprisonment, Plus Obligatory Disqualification & Compulsory Re-Testing

Learning Points – Causing Death By Dangerous Driving

Who Must Die?

- The **person who dies** as a result of the act of dangerous driving must be a **person other than the defendant.**

Foetuses

- The person may include a foetus that is injured in the womb as a result of the act of dangerous driving and later dies after birth having lead an independent existence - *McCluskey v HM Advocate* [1989] SLT 175.

The Cause Of Death

- The act of dangerous driving does **not** need to be the **sole** or **major cause of the death.**
- The act of dangerous driving need only be a **contributory cause of death** which was more than a mere trifling cause of death – *R v Hennigan* [1971] 3 All RE 133.

Exam Trip Up

- It is **not** a **defence** for the driver to assert that they **did not intend** to drive dangerously.

Exam Trip Up

- The **same standards** apply to **all drivers** irrespective of their experience.

Exam Trip Up

- Section 2 of the Road Traffic Act 1988 states that where the dangerous driving leads to an accident, the court **may allow a police officer who is an expert in collision investigation of accidents to give evidence of opinion as to the cause of that accident** - *R v Oakley* [1979] RTR 417).

Exam Trip Up

- In the case of *Milton v CPS* [2007] EWCH 532, the administrative court held that the fact that the driver was a grade 1 advanced police driver was a circumstance which it was necessary to take into account pursuant to Sec.2A (3) – i.e. in determining whether or not the driving fell far below the required standard.
- A highly skilled and highly trained driver is entitled to have those skills and abilities taken into account, when considering whether or not the driving was dangerous.

Checklist - Dangerous Driving & Causing Death By Dangerous Driving

Step 1	Did the accused **drive** an **MPV?**	If no – no offence. If yes – go to step 2.
Step 2	Was the MPV **driven** on either a **road** or **public place?**	If no – no offence. If yes – go to step 3.
Step 3	Was the MPV **driven dangerously**?	If no – no offence. If yes - guilty of **dangerous driving**. Check step 4 to see if guilty of causing death by dangerous driving.
Step 4	Was the act of dangerous driving a **contributory cause of the death** of a person other than the driver?	If no – only guilty of **dangerous driving**. If yes – guilty of **causing death by dangerous driving.**

C - Careless Or Inconsiderate Driving, Causing Death By Careless Driving Whilst Unfit Through Drink Or Drugs, Causing Death By Careless Driving Of A Motor Vehicle Whilst Over The Alcohol Limit & Causing Death By Careless Driving & Fails To Provide A Specimen

Careless Or Inconsiderate Driving	Causing Death By Careless Driving Whilst Unfit Through Drink Or Drugs	Causing Death By Careless Driving Of A Motor Vehicle Whilst Over The Alcohol Limit	Causing Death By Careless Driving Of A Motor Vehicle & Fails To Provide A Specimen
Section 3 Road Traffic Act 1988	**Section 3A(1)(a) Road Traffic Act 1988**	**Section 3A(1)(b) Road Traffic Act 1988**	**Section 3A(1)(c) Road Traffic Act 1988**
A person commits an offence of **careless or inconsiderate driving** if they: ☐ **Drive** an **MPV;** ☐ On either: ■ A **road;** or ■ Other **public place;** ☐ **Without** either: ■ **Due care and attention;** or ■ **Reasonable consideration** for other road users.	It is an offence to: ☐ **Cause** the **death** of another human being; ☐ By **driving** an **MPV;** ☐ On either: ■ A **road**; or ■ Other **public place**; ☐ **Without** either: ■ **Due care and attention;** or ■ **Reasonable consideration** for other road users; and ☐ They are **unfit** through **drink** or **drugs.**	It is an offence to: ☐ **Cause** the **death** of another human being; ☐ By **driving** a **motor vehicle;** ☐ On either: ■ A **road**; or ■ Other **public place**; ☐ **Without** either: ■ **Due care and attention;** or ■ **Reasonable consideration** for other road users; and ☐ The proportion of **alcohol** in their **breath/blood/urine exceeds the limit.**	It is an offence to: ☐ **Cause** the **death** of another human being; ☐ By **driving** a **motor vehicle;** ☐ On either: ■ A **road**; or ■ Other **public place**; ☐ **Without** either: ■ **Due care and attention;** or ■ **Reasonable consideration** for other road users; and ☐ **Fail** to provide an **evidentiary specimen** within **18 hours** of the act of driving that caused the death; and ☐ They did not have a **reasonable excuse.** NB - Not a preliminary breath test.

Section 3 Road Traffic Act 1988	Section 3A(1)(a) Road Traffic Act 1988	Section 3A(1)(b) Road Traffic Act 1988	Section 3A(1)(c) Road Traffic Act 1988
Summary Only Offence Penalty In The Magistrates Court – Fine & Discretionary Disqualification	Indictable Only Offence Penalty In The Crown Court - Fourteen Years Imprisonment & Obligatory Disqualification (Minimum Of 2 Years)	Indictable Only Offence Penalty In The Crown Court - Fourteen Years Imprisonment & Obligatory Disqualification (Minimum Of 2 Years)	Indictable Only Offence Penalty In The Crown Court - Fourteen Years Imprisonment & Obligatory Disqualification (Minimum Of 2 Years)

Learning Points Applicable To All 4 Offences

Definition Of Due Care And Attention

Due care and attention refers to driving which falls **below** the **standards** expected of a **driver** who is **both**:

Characteristic 1	Characteristic 2
Competent.	**Careful.**

Due Care And Attention – An Objective Test

- The test is a **question of fact** – taking into consideration the surrounding circumstances at the time of driving.
- It is **not necessary** to **prove** that the accused was **aware** that their driving had fallen **below** the **standards** expected of a **driver** who is both **competent** and **careful** – i.e. the test is **objective.**

Definition Of Reasonable Consideration

- An absence of reasonable consideration will involve persons ***actually*** **being inconvenienced by the driving.**
- For example – it will be necessary to prove that a person driving through a puddle **actually splashed** and therefore **inconvenienced** a passer-by – *Pawley v Wharldall* [1965] 2 All ER 757.

What Is Driven?

The offences relate to the driving of different modes of transport:	
Mechanically Propelled Vehicle	**Motor Vehicle**
■ Careless & Inconsiderate Driving – Section 3 ■ Causing Death By Careless Driving Whilst Unfit Through Drink Or Drugs – Section 3A(1)(a)	■ Causing Death By Careless Driving Of A Motor Vehicle Whilst Over The Alcohol Limit – Section 3A(1)(b) ■ Causing Death By Careless Driving Of A Motor Vehicle & Fails To Provide A Specimen – Section 3A(1)(c)

Exam Trip Up

- A person is guilty of driving without due care and attention if the **way they drive falls below what would be expected of a competent and careful driver.**
- The offence will be complete if it is proven that the defendant **departed from that standard** and that their actions were **'voluntary'**.
- There is **no onus** on the prosecution to **prove** any **knowledge or awareness** that their **driving fell below the expected standard or driving** - *R v Lawrence* [1981] RTR 217.

Exam Trip Up

- In the case of *Henderson v Jones* [1955] 119 JP 304, it was held that a driver who **falls asleep at the wheel** will be **guilty of careless driving.**
- If however there is no other supporting evidence and the testimony of this fact arises from the driver alone, this will be inadequate evidence to support a charge of careless driving.

Checklist – Section 3 & Section 3A(1)(a)

Step 1	Did the person drive a **mechanically propelled vehicle (MPV)?**	If no – no offence. If yes – go to step 2.
Step 2	Was the MPV **driven** on a **road** or **public place**?	If no – no offence. If yes – go to step 3.
Step 3	Was the MPV driven **without** either: ■ **Due care and attention;** or ■ **Reasonable consideration** for other road users.	If no – no offence. If yes - guilty of careless or inconsiderate driving. Check step 4 to see if guilty of causing death by careless or inconsiderate driving.
Step 4	Was the act of driving a **contributory cause** of the **death** of a person other than the driver?	If no - guilty of **careless or inconsiderate driving.** If yes – go to step 5.
Step 5	Was the driver **unfit** through either **drink** or **drugs?**	If no - guilty of **careless or inconsiderate driving.** If yes - guilty of **causing death by careless or inconsiderate driving.**

Checklist – Section 3A(1)(b) & Section 3A(1)(c)

Step 1	Did the person drive a **motor vehicle**?	If no – no offence. If yes – go to step 2.
Step 2	Was the motor vehicle driven on a **road** or **public place?**	If no – no offence. If yes – go to step 3.
Step 3	Was the motor vehicle driven **without** either: ■ **Due care and attention;** or ■ **Reasonable consideration** for other road users.	If no – no offence. If yes - guilty of **careless or inconsiderate driving.** Check step 4 to see if guilty of causing death by careless or inconsiderate driving.

Step 4	Was the act of **driving** a **contributory cause** of the **death** of a person other than the driver?		If no - guilty of **careless or inconsiderate driving.** If yes – go to step 5.
Step 5	Was the proportion of **alcohol** in the driver's **breath/blood/urine** in **excess** of the legal **limit?**	Did the driver f**ail** to provide an **evidentiary specimen** within **18 hours** of the act of driving that caused the death without a **reasonable excuse?**	If no - guilty of **careless or inconsiderate driving.** If yes - guilty of **causing death by careless or inconsiderate driving**.

Exam Trip Up

- **Some person** must be shown to have been **inconvenienced** as a result of the defendant's actions - *Dilks v Bowman-Shaw* [1981] RTR 4.
- Persons using the road or public place includes **pedestrians** who are **deliberately sprayed with water** - *Pawley v Wharldall* [1965] 2 All ER 757,

D – Causing Death By Careless Or Inconsiderate Driving

Section 2B Road Traffic Act 1988
Either Way Offence
Penalty In The Crown Court – 5 Years Imprisonment And Or A Fine
Penalty In The Magistrates Court – 12 Months Imprisonment And Obligatory Disqualification

A person commits an offence if they **cause the death of another person** by **driving a mechanically propelled vehicle (MPV)** on **either:**	
A **road**	A **public place**
...**either**:	
Without **due care and attention**.	Without **consideration** for other persons using the road or place.

Learning Points

- Note that this offence relates to the **wider definition** of a **Mechanically Propelled Vehicle (MPV).**
- Note that the driving can take place on a **wider location** of <u>either</u> a **road** or a **public place.**

E – Causing Death By Driving Whilst Either Unlicensed, Disqualified, Or Uninsured

Section 3ZB Road Traffic Act 1988
Either Way Offence
Penalty In The Crown Court – 2 Years Imprisonment And Or A Fine
Penalty In The Magistrates Court – 12 Months Imprisonment And Obligatory Disqualification

A person commits an offence if they **cause the death of another person** by **driving a motor vehicle** on a **road** – and at the time of driving they were <u>**either:**</u>		
Driving otherwise than in accordance with a **license.**	Driving whist **disqualified.**	Driving whist **uninsured** or **unsecured against 3rd party risk**.

Learning Points

- Note that this offence relates to the **narrower definition** of a **Motor Vehicle - (not an MPV).**
- Note that the driving can take place on a **narrower location** of <u>only</u> a **road - (not a public place).**
- The offence does not require anything to be wrong with the actual quality of driving.
- All that is required is that the driving caused the death and they were unlicensed, disqualified or uninsured at the time.

F - Failing To Stop

Section 59(1) Police Reform Act 2002
Summary Only Offence
Penalty In The Magistrates Court – A Fine

- A person that fails to comply with an order under subsection (3)(A) is guilty of an offence.

Exam Trip Ups

- The order relates to the person driving.
- If there is to be a prosecution it is necessary to display that the order was properly given - i.e. that the person giving the order had the authority to do so.
- The stopping must be for a sufficient duration to enable the officer to exercise whatever additional powers are appropriate - *Lodwick v Sanders* [1985] 1 All ER 577.

G – Driving A Motor Vehicle On A Road Whilst Using A Hand Held Mobile Phone

Section 41D Road Traffic Act 1988
Summary Offence
Fine, 3 Points & Discretionary Disqualification

There are 3 offences:		
Offence 1	**Offence 2**	**Offence 3**
Driving Themselves	**Causing / Permitting A Driver**	**Supervising Learner Drivers**
No person shall drive a motor vehicle on a road if they are using a hand held mobile phone.	No person shall cause or permit any other person to drive a motor vehicle on a road whilst that person is using a hand held mobile phone.	No person shall supervise the driving of a provisional licence holder whilst they are on a hand held mobile phone.

What Is A Hand Held Mobile Phone

- A mobile phone will be hand held if it is being held at some point during the making or receiving of a call.

Driving

- The definition of driving is wide and includes drivers who have pulled over to the side of the road to take a call with the engine still running.

Defence

A person will have a **defence** if all of the following steps are satisfied:		
Step 1	**Step 2**	**Step 3**
They used the phone to call the **emergency services (999 call).**	The 999 call was made in **response to an emergency**.	It is **unsafe** or **impracticable** to **cease driving** to make the call.

Road Policing
Subject 2: Drink Drugs & Driving

A – Unfit Through Drink Or Drugs & Driving Over The Prescribed Limit

There are **2 offences:**	
Unfitness Through Drink Or Drugs	**Driving Over The Prescribed Limit**
Section 4 Road Traffic Act 1988	**Section 5 Road Traffic Act 1988**
It is an offence for a person: ☐ To either: ■ **Drive;** ■ **Attempt** to drive; or ■ Be **in charge** of; ☐ A **MPV;** ☐ On either a: ■ **Road;** or ■ **Public place;** ☐ If they are **unfit** through either: ■ **Drink;** or ■ **Drugs.**	It is an offence for a person: ☐ To either: ■ **Drive;** ■ **Attempt** to drive; ■ Be **in charge;** ☐ Of a **motor vehicle;** ☐ On either a: ■ **Road;** or ■ **Public place;** ☐ After consuming so much **alcohol;** (NB – not drugs). ☐ That the proportion of it in their **breath/blood/urine exceeds the limit.**
Summary Only Offence Penalty In The Magistrates Court: 6 Months Imprisonment And / Or A Fine Plus Obligatory Disqualification	Summary Only Offence Penalty In The Magistrates Court: 3 Months Imprisonment And / Or A Fine Plus Discretionary Disqualification

Learning Points: Unfitness Through Drink Or Drugs – Section 4 Road Traffic Act 1988

Driving / Attempting To Drive / Being In Charge

There are in essence **3 separate offences:**		
Offence 1	**Offence 2**	**Offence 3**
Driving.	Attempting to drive.	Being in charge.

Proving Driving / Attempting To Drive / Being In Charge

- The case of *R (On the Application of Huntley) v DPP* [2004] EWHC 870 established that a mere **suspicion** that the person was either **driving, attempting to drive, or in charge** of the vehicle will be **insufficient.**

An MPV

- Note that the **section 4** offence relates to an **MPV.**
- Whereas the **section 5** offence relates to a **motor vehicle.**

On A Road Or Public Place

- Watch out for questions involving an MPV on **private land – no offence.**
- Note that both sections 4 and 5 relate to driving on a **road** or **public place.**

It Is Necessary To Prove That The Person Was Unfit By Virtue of Either Drink Or Drugs

- Note that the **section 4** offence relates to **both**:
  - ☐ **Drink**; or
  - ☐ **Drugs.**
- Whereas the **section 5** offence relates **only** to excess **alcohol** – NB **not drugs.**

How Can Unfitness Be Proven?

Evidence of unfitness can come from __either:__	
Source 1	**Source 2**
A **lay** witness – *R v Lanfear* [1968] 2 QB 77.	An **expert** witness.

Permitted Evidence By Lay Witnesses

Fitness	Ability To Drive
A lay witness **can** give evidence that the person was **unfit.** There is **no need** for **expert evidence** on whether the person was unfit.	Lay witnesses **cannot** give evidence as to the defendant's **ability to drive.**

It Is Not Necessary To Prove Any Quantity Of Alcohol Or Drugs In The Person's System

- Under section 4 it is **not necessary** to **prove any quantity of alcohol or drugs** in the defendant's system – **only unfitness.**
- In the real world you are going to proceed to prove the quantity of alcohol or drugs - however for the purposes of the exam this is **not necessary**.
- Note how this **contrasts** with the **section 5** offence which relates to **excess alcohol** where **proof** will be required.

Exam Trip Up – Suspicion Of Unfitness After A Negative Breath Test Due To The Suspect Physically Appearing To Be Unfit

- The case of *DPP v Robertson* [2002] RTR 383, established that:
  - ☐ If a person provides a **negative breath test;** and
  - ☐ Is then nevertheless seen displaying physical **behaviour** that suggests that they are **unfit** – e.g. slurring, staggering away, etc;
  - ☐ Then they will still be guilty of the offence.

Defence: When Will A Person Not Be In Charge – Section 4(3) Road Traffic Act 1988

A person will **not be in charge** if they prove that - at the time, the circumstances were such that there was **no likelihood** of them **driving, so long as they remained unfit** through **either:**	
Drink.	**Drugs.**

Checklist - Unfitness Through Drink Or Drugs

Step 1	■ Did a person either: ☐ **Drive** an **MPV**? ☐ **Attempt to drive** an **MPV**? ■ Were they **in charge** of an **MPV**?	If no – no offence. If yes – go to step 2.
Step 2	Were they on either: ■ **Road;** or ■ **Public place**?	If no – no offence. If yes – go to step 3.
Step 3	Were they **unfit** though either: ■ **Drink**; or ■ **Drugs**?	If no – no offence. If yes – guilty unless specific defence to being carried in step 4 is established.
Step 4	Was there **no likelihood** of them **driving so long as they remained unfit** through either **drink** or **drugs?**	If yes – no offence. If no – guilty.

Learning Points: Driving Over The Prescribed Limit – Section 5 Road Traffic Act 1988

Driving / Attempting To Drive / Being In Charge

There are in essence **3 separate offences**:		
Offence 1	**Offence 2**	**Offence 3**
Driving.	**Attempting to drive.**	**Being in charge.**

A Motor Vehicle

- Note that the **section 5** offence relates to a **motor vehicle.**
- Whereas the **section 4** offence relates to an **MPV.**

On A Road Or Public Place

- Watch out for questions involving an MPV on **private land** – **no offence.**

With Excess Alcohol In Their Blood, Breath, Or Urine - Legal Limits – Section 11(2) RTA 1988

	Volume In Sample (NB – focus on whether micrograms or milligrams)	**Millilitres (for all)**
Breath	**35 micrograms**	In **100 millilitres** of breath
Blood	**80 milligrams**	In **100 millilitres** of blood
Urine	**107 milligrams**	In **100 millilitres** of urine

Memory Aid

- Note how the figures in each instance all **add up to 8.**
  - ☐ 3 + 5 = **8**
  - ☐ 8 + 0 = **8**
  - ☐ 1 + 0 + 7 = **8**

Exam Trip Up

- Questions in recent years have related to the **words surrounding the numbers** – you need to learn parrot fashion whether each figure relates to:
  - ☐ **Micrograms – breath;** or
  - ☐ **Milligrams – blood & urine.**

Defence - Driving Over The Prescribed Limit

- A person will not be guilty if they prove that at the time the circumstances were such that there was **no likelihood** of them **driving so long as the proportion of alcohol in their system exceeds the maximum.**

High Risk Offender Scheme

- The **High Risk Offender Scheme** generally applies to offenders who are **convicted of relevant offences** and **at the time** were either:
  - ☐ **More than two and a half times over the prescribed limit**; or
  - ☐ The conviction is their **second (or more) in ten years**.
- Any offenders who fall within the criteria of the HROS will be required to undergo a **medical test prior to being allowed to regain their driver's licence** after the disqualification term has elapsed.

Checklist – Driving Over The Prescribed Limit

Step 1	■ Did a person either: ☐ **Drive** a **<u>motor vehicle</u>**? ☐ **Attempt** to drive a **<u>motor vehicle</u>**? ■ Were they **in charge** of a **<u>motor vehicle</u>**?	If no – no offence. If yes – go to step 2.
Step 2	Were they on either: ■ **Road**; or ■ **Public place**?	If no – no offence. If yes – go to step 3.

Step 3	Were they in **excess of the alcohol limit**?	If no – no offence. If yes – guilty unless specific defence to being carried in step 4 is established.
Step 4	Was there **no likelihood** of them **driving so long as they remained in excess of the alcohol limit?**	If yes – no offence. If no – guilty.

Police Officers Convicted Of Drink Driving

- The **normal punishment** which can be expected when police officers are convicted of drink driving, irrespective of whether the matter took place when the officer was on or off duty would be **dismissal,** or a **requirement to resign.**
- The guidance issued to Chief Constables by the home secretary **does not stipulate that the officer must be dismissed or required to resign.**
- Even so, the punishment would normally be one of the foregoing options and would be a decision for the Chief Officer.

B - Testing A Suspect

There are 2 forms of tests:	
Preliminary Tests	**Evidentiary Tests**

C - Preliminary Tests

1 – Non-Accident Situations – Section 6 Road Traffic Act 1988

There are **3 different situations** justifying the request for a person to engage in a preliminary test in **non accident situations:**

Present Tense Driving/Attempt/In Charge	Past Tense Driving/Attempt/In Charge	Either Present & Past Tense Driving/Attempt/In Charge
Section 6(2)	**Section 6(3)**	**Section 6(4)**

In **all 3 instances** a **constable** can **request** a person to engage in a preliminary breath test if they reasonably **suspect** that the person:

Section 6(2)

- Either:
  - Is **(currently)** driving;
  - Is **(currently)** attempting to drive;
  - Is **(currently)** in charge;
- Of a **motor vehicle** (not MPV) on either a:
  - **Road;** or
  - **Public place**;

AND

- Either:
  - Has **alcohol** in their body;
  - Has a **drug** in their body; or
  - Is under the influence of a **drug (NB not alcohol).**

Section 6(3)

- Either:
  - Has **(in the past)** been driving;
  - Has **(in the past)** been attempting to drive;
  - Has **(in the past)** been in charge;
- Of a **motor vehicle** (not MPV) on either a:
  - **Road;** or
  - **Public place**;

AND

- Either:
  - While having **alcohol** in their body;
  - While having a **drug** in their body; or
  - While **unfit** to drive because of a **drug (NB not alcohol).**

AND

- **Still** (at the time of the request) either:
  - Has alcohol in their body;
  - Has the drug in their body;
  - Is under the influence of the drug.

Section 6(4)

- Either:
  - Is **(currently)** driving;
  - Is **(currently)** attempting to drive;
  - Is **(currently)** in charge;

OR

- Either:
  - Has **(in the past)** been driving;
  - Has **(in the past)** been attempting to drive;
  - Has **(in the past)** been in charge;
- Of a **motor vehicle** (not MPV) on either a:
  - **Road**; or
  - **Public place**;

AND

- Has committed a **traffic offence** while the vehicle was **in motion**.

Where May The Reasonable Suspicion Emanate From?

The **reasonable suspicion** of the constable making the requirement for the suspect to engage in a preliminary breath test may **emanate from** either:

Source 1	Source 2	Source 3
The constable's own observations.	The observations of another constable. *Erskine v Hollin* [1971] RTR 199	Information provided by a member of the public. *DPP v Wilson* [1991] RTR 284

Exam Trip Up

- Note the differing mental element of the constable when requesting a preliminary test after an accident – they will ***"believe"*** (see below).

Need The Officer Be In Uniform?

The Constable Requesting The Suspect To Provide A Preliminary Test	The Constable Administering The Preliminary Test
Does **not** have to be in uniform.	**Must** be in uniform.

When Will An Officer Be Deemed To Be In Uniform?

- This is a **question of fact** – a constable will be deemed to be in uniform if they can be easily identified by their dress.

Exam Trip Up

- Watch out for questions involving the requesting officer **without a helmet on** – they will still be "in uniform" – *Wallwork v Giles* [1970] RTR 117.

Exam Trip Up

- Note the **contrasting uniform provisions** in relation to requests for a preliminary test in **accident situations** (see below).
- Under section 6 (6) of the Road Traffic Act 1988, a person's attitude and conduct after being required to give a breath specimen may be sufficient to make out the offence and evidence of the officer witnessing the attitude or conduct may suffice as proof that it amounted to a failure or refusal.
- In the event that a person clearly does something which amounts to a refusal to provide a preliminary test, the offence will be made out even though the officer did not produce a device for doing so - *DPP v Swan* [2004] EWHC 2432.

2 – Preliminary Tests - Accident Situations

<table>
<tr><td colspan="2">A constable may request a person to provide a preliminary test if <u>both</u>:</td></tr>
<tr><th>Step 1</th><th>Step 2</th></tr>
<tr><td>■ They <u>know</u> (for a fact) that an accident occurred owing to the presence of a motor vehicle on a:
☐ Road; or
☐ Public place.</td><td>■ They reasonably <u>believe</u> that the person was either:
☐ Driving;
☐ Attempting to drive;
☐ In charge of;
■ The vehicle at the time of the accident.</td></tr>
</table>

Need The Officer Making The Requirement For A Preliminary Test Be In Uniform?

- **No.**

The Range Of Preliminary Tests

There are **3 different forms** of **preliminary tests**:		
Preliminary Breath Tests Section 6A	**Preliminary Impairment Tests Section 6B**	**Preliminary Drugs Tests Section 6C**
Can **only** be administered **at or near** the place where the requirement to co-operate was made.	Can be administered either: ■ **At or near** the place where the requirement to co-operate was made; or ■ If **expedient** - at a specified **police station.**	Can be administered either: ■ **At or near** the place where the requirement to co-operate was made; or ■ If **expedient** - at a specified **police station.**

Exam Trip Up

- Note the **more limited location** at which a **breath test** can be conducted in comparison with impairment tests and drugs tests.

When Can A Preliminary Breath Test Be Carried Out At A Police Station?

- The only occasion where a preliminary breath test can be conducted at a police station after an **accident** is when **the constable who imposes the requirement thinks it expedient to carry the test out at a police station specified by them.**

- As can be seen from the above table all the other preliminary tests can be routinely carried out at the station and at the roadside.

Failure To Co-operate With A Request For A Preliminary Test

Section 6(6) Road Traffic Act 1988
Summary Offence
Fine & Discretionary Disqualification

A person will commit an offence if **both**:	
Step 1	**Step 2**
Without a **reasonable excuse...**	...they **fail** or **refuse** to **co-operate** with a properly made request for a preliminary test.
Examples of a **reasonable excuse** include: ■ The person is physically unable to conduct the test. ■ Conducting the test would involve a substantial risk to their health.	For example: **Refusal** – an **outright rejection** of the test as evidenced by **words** or **conduct**. **Failure** – either: ■ Their **actions** are **insufficient** to allow the test or analysis to be carried out. e.g. not just blow, but blow enough to provide a reliable reading. ■ Having been **requested to wait** for the apparatus to be brought to the scene – they **fail to wait** for a **reasonable period of time** – *R v Wagner* [1970] Crim LR 535.

The Request For The Preliminary Sample Must Be Properly Made - Trespassing

- An officer **trespassing** on the defendant's property is not entitled to request a breath test – *R v Fox* [1986] AC 281.

Exam Trip Up

- Generally, **failing to follow key instructions of the manufacturer** such as assembling the tube on a breathalyser or allowing the driver to smoke immediately before taking the test – means that the **person will not have provided a preliminary test.**

- Consequently they may be **asked to provide another preliminary test**.
- **Refusing** to do so will be an **offence** - *DPP v Carey* [1969] 3 All ER 1662.
- Furthermore, an **innocent failure** by a police officer to **follow the manufacturer's instructions** should not be deemed to render either the **test** or any subsequent **arrest unlawful** - *DPP v Kay* [1999] RTR 109.

Police Powers Of Entry To Request A Preliminary Test & To Arrest Following An Accident – Section 6E(1) Road Traffic Act 1988

Step 1	■ Does a constable **know (for a fact)** that there has been an **accident?**
Step 2	■ Does the constable reasonably **believe** that the person either: ☐ Had been **driving;** ☐ Had been **attempting** to drive; ☐ Was **in charge** of; ■ A **motor vehicle.**
Step 3	■ Does the constable reasonably **suspect** that the **accident** involved an **injury** to either: ☐ The **driver**; or ☐ **Any other person**.
Step 4	■ If the answer is **yes to all these questions** - the constable ***may*** **enter any place** (using **reasonable force** if necessary) for the purpose of either:

Preliminary Test	Arrest For Over The Limit	Arrest For Failure To Co-operate In Providing A Preliminary Test
Imposing a **requirement** for a **preliminary test.**	**Arresting** a person if as a **result** of a **preliminary test** the officer reasonably **suspects** that the proportion of alcohol in their breath or blood **exceeds** the limits.	**Arresting** a person for **failing to co-operate** with a **preliminary test** where the officer reasonably **suspects** that the person either: ■ Has alcohol in their body; ■ Has drugs in their body; or ■ Is under the influence of drugs.

Learning Point

- Focus on how the mental element decreases at each stage of the test:

Know
I
Believe
I
Suspect

Need The Constable Be In Uniform To Arrest?

- No.

D - Evidentiary Specimens – Section 7 Road Traffic Act 1988

<table>
<tr><td colspan="3">These are the specimens that will be relied upon at court as evidence and fall into 3 categories:</td></tr>
<tr><td>Breath</td><td>Urine</td><td>Blood</td></tr>
<tr><td>Location Of The Requirement
The requirement can be made at either:
■ Hospital;
■ Police station;
■ At or near the place the request for the preliminary test in relation to an accident was made or administered - (NB must be in uniform).</td><td colspan="2">Location Of The Requirement
The requirement can be made at either:
■ Hospital;
■ Police station.
NB – Not at or near place the request for the preliminary test in relation to an accident was made or administered</td></tr>
</table>

1 - Evidentiary Specimens At A Police Station

The Default Option – Evidentiary Specimens Of Breath

- As a **general rule** the suspect will be requested to provide an evidentiary specimen of **breath** at a **police station.**
- The **exceptional circumstances** where either **blood or urine** may be requested can be found in section 7(3) Road Traffic Act 1988 (see below).
- As required by section16 of The Road Traffic Offenders Act 1988, the **defendant must be provided with a copy of any statement produced by a machine used for the breath test procedure.**
- Following the case of *Chief Constable of Surrey v Wickens* [1985] RTR 277, there is **no requirement** for any copy provided to the defendant to be **signed by any police officer.**

Specimens Of Breath

A specimen of **breath** will include **either**:		
Mouth alcohol.	Reflux of stomach content.	Deep lung air.

How Many Specimens Of Breath Will Be Required?

The suspect will be required to supply **2 specimens of breath**:	
Lower Reading	**Higher Reading**
The specimen with the **lower reading** will be **used** for **evidentiary purposes**.	The specimen with the **higher reading** will be **disregarded.**

What Happens If The Suspect Only Provides 1 Specimen Of Breath?

- If the suspect only provides **1 sample** then they will be guilty of a **failure to provide**.

Options Available Where The Lower Reading Is Not More Than 50 Micrograms Of Alcohol In 100 Millilitres Of Breath – Section 8 Road Traffic Act 1988

Where a suspect has **blown** on their **lower reading 50 micrograms or less** they have **2 options** - **either**:	
Option 1	**Option 2**
Stick with the **lower reading of breath** as their evidentiary specimen.	**Disregard** the **lower reading breath** specimen and instead **replace** the specimen with either **blood** or **urine**.

Exam Trip Up

- Once the suspect goes ahead with the specimen of blood or urine it will **not be possible to revert back to the disregarded specimen of breath.**
- This will even be the case where the **blood specimen** turns out to be **unsuitable for analysis** – *Archbold v Jones* [1985] Crim LR 740.

Memory Aid

- In the above circumstances, perhaps the easiest way to remember is - '*when there's a flaw, there is no second chance for the law'!*

Exam Trip Up

- Once the suspect goes ahead with the rejection of the lower breath reading – it will be the **choice of the constable** whether to opt for **blood or urine** (see below).

Requiring A Specimen Of Breath At A Police Station After Having Already Made The Requirement Elsewhere

- If a **request** for an **evidentiary breath specimen** has already **previously been made at a place other than a police station** (i.e. hospital or place where the preliminary test was requested);
- It will still be possible to make a **further request** for an evidentiary breath specimen **at a police station** provided **either:**

Situation 1 – Specimen Not Taken	Situation 2 – Specimen Taken But Unreliable
After making the request the evidentiary specimen was not taken at the location away from the police station because either: ■ The **device** was **not available**; or ■ It was **not practicable** to use the device.	After making the request the evidentiary specimen was taken at the location away from the police station but the constable reasonably believes the device has produced an **unreliable result.**

Exceptional Circumstances Where Blood Or Urine May Be Requested At A Police Station – Section 7(3) Road Traffic Act 1988

Blood or **urine** will only be obtained as an alternative to breath **at a police station** where **either**:

Situation 1	Situation 2	Situation 3	Situation 4	Situation 5
Medical Reason	**Intoximeter Unavailable / Impractical**	**Intoximeter Unreliable**	**Believe Drug In System**	**Medical Advice Re Drugs**
The constable has reasonable cause to **believe** that for **medical reasons** a specimen of breath either: ■ **Cannot** be provided; or ■ **Should not** be requested.	Specimens of breath have not been obtained elsewhere and an **intoximeter** is either: ■ **Not available**; or ■ It is **not practicable to use.**	Specimens of breath have been obtained but the constable has reasonable cause to **believe** that the intoximeter produced an **unreliable reading.**	After a preliminary drugs test the constable has reasonable cause to **believe** that they have a **drug in their system.**	The constable has been advised by a **medical practitioner** that the person's condition might be due to a **drug.**

NB – If any of the 5 situations apply – the **request for urine or blood can still be made even if:**

- A **requirement** has been **made** to provide **2 specimens of breath**; or
- In light of the requirement - **2 or more samples of breath have been provided**.

Medical Reason

- There is no need to seek the advice of a medical practitioner – all the officer has to do is prove that there are objective facts available that could form the basis of a belief – *Dempsey v Catton* [1986] RTR 194.
- The case of *Young v DPP* [1992] RTR 328 established that being too drunk to provide a breath specimen will be a medical reason.

- The case of *Andrews v DPP* [1992] RTR established that the medical advice can be given over the phone if necessary.

- Evidently, the ideal scenario would be for the doctor to attend in person, yet this would undoubtedly cause unnecessary delays in securing evidence. Whatever the content of the conversation between the custody officer and the doctor, the nucleus would be recorded on the defendant's custody record.

Intoximeter Unavailable

- An intoximeter will be **unavailable** if it is **uncalibrated.**

- If as a result an evidentiary specimen of urine or blood is obtained – the urine or blood must be used and it will not be possible to revert back to breath.

Not Practicable To Use The Intoximeter

- It will **not be practicable** to use the intoximeter where there is **no trained operator** available.

Intoxilizer Unreliable

- In the case of *DPP v Denny* [1990] RTR 417, it was established that:

    - ☐ If the **intoxilizer is faulty** at the **initial police station**;

    - ☐ The defendant can be **transferred to another police station where another intoxilizer is available;**

    - ☐ **Even though 2 specimens have already been given on the inaccurate machine.**

Medical Advice Re Drugs

- The power to require blood or urine under this head can only be utilised if a **medical practitioner** has **advised** that the suspect's condition relates to drugs.

- If such advice has been provided - it will only be permissible to request the blood or urine in relation to offences of either:

    - ☐ **Being unfit**; or

    - ☐ **Causing death by careless driving whilst under the influence of drink or drugs.**

- When such medical advice is sought, the doctor must give the officer a clear verbal statement to the effect that the driver's condition was due to some drug before the power arises - *Cole v DPP* [1988] RTR 224.

Action To Be Taken If Blood Or Urine Is To Be Requested At A Police Station – Section 7(4) & 7(4)(A)

The case of DPP v Warren [1993] AC 319 established that a **constable** will have the power to decide **both**:

Decision 1	Decision 2
Which of the 2 options of **blood** or **urine** they will choose to request from the suspect.	If **blood** is chosen – **who will take** the specimen.

Learning Point

- Even though a constable may wish to require the evidentiary specimen via blood the outcome of whether they will be able to do so will depend upon:
  - Any reasonable medical reason for not doing so being raised by the accused; and
  - Any objections from a registered medical practitioner or health care professional based upon a medical reason.

Exam Trip Up

- An alleged fear of needles by the driver is a relevant consideration when making the decision to request whether a sample of blood or urine should be taken - *DPP v Jackson* [1998] 3 WLR 514; *Stanley v DPP* [1998] 3 WLR 514 and also *Johnson v West Yorkshire Metropolitan Police* [1986] RTR 167.

The Process To Be Followed When The Constable Is To Request An Evidentiary Sample Of Blood Or Urine

<table>
<tr><td>Step 1</td><td colspan="2">The constable must warn the suspect that the failure to provide an evidentiary specimen will result in prosecution for an offence.</td></tr>
<tr><td>Step 2</td><td>Where An Evidentiary Breath Specimen Of 50 Or Less Has Been Obtained

The constable must explain that the specimen of breath containing the lower proportion of alcohol did not exceed 50 micrograms in 100 millilitres of breath.</td><td>Where No Evidentiary Breath Specimen Has Been Obtained

The constable must explain the reasons why the standard option of an evidentiary specimen of breath will not be requested (via one of the criteria in section 7(3).</td></tr>
<tr><td>Step 3</td><td colspan="2">The constable must ask the suspect whether there are any medical reasons why a particular specimen could not or should not be taken.</td></tr>
<tr><td>Step 4</td><td colspan="2">The suspect should in response raise any relevant medical conditions:
■ If the medical grounds are reasonable - the constable must instead offer urine.
■ If the medical grounds are unreasonable – the constable will be able to obtain a sample of blood subject to any objections on medical grounds being raised by a registered medical practitioner or health care professional.</td></tr>
<tr><td>Step 5</td><td colspan="2">■ The request for an evidentiary sample of blood will be made unless the:
☐ Registered medical practitioner; or
☐ Registered health care professional;
■ Who is asked to take the blood forms the opinion that the specimen cannot / should not be taken for medical reasons.
■ If such medical objections are raised – a specimen of urine will be obtained instead.</td></tr>
</table>

Exam Trip Up

- NB – If the decision is initially taken by a registered health care professional, they can be overruled by a registered medical practitioner.

Exam Trip Up

- Once the defendant elects to provide a further sample (both blood or urine) there is no longer a reliance on the breath sample and no requirement for the prosecution to demonstrate that the device used to obtain the breath sample was reliable or of an approved type - see *Wright v DPP* [2005] EWHC 1211.

Procedure For Taking Evidentiary Specimens Of Urine

Who Can Obtain The Specimen?

- **Specimens of urine** can be **taken** by an **officer.**
- The administrative court has held that there is **no free-standing right** either under the 1988 Act or at common law for the **defendant to be informed of their entitlement to a part of the sample** - see *Campbell v DPP* [2003] Crim LR 118).
- Although the specimen must be divided 'at the time', there is **no need** for it to be **done in the defendant's presence** - *DPP* v *Elstob* [1992] Crim LR 518).

How Many Specimens Must Be Taken?

- **2 distinct specimens** must be taken from **2 separate acts of urination** - (as opposed to 2 specimens being taken during 1 act of urination).

How Long Does The Suspect Have To Provide The 2 Specimens Of Urine?

- The suspect must be given the **opportunity to provide the urine within an hour long period.**
- The **hour** within which the specimens must be produced **begins from the time that the request is made** (and not between the 1st and 2nd samples being provided).
- The importance of the one hour period was to make the length of time available to the driver to provide a specimen a finite period. Therefore anyone who does not provide a sample within that time could be charged with failure to supply a sample.
- An officer is **not obliged to extend the time** in which a sample could be supplied, however they **could do so** and such an **extension will not cause the analysis of the specimen to be inadmissible** - *DPP v Baldwin* 2000 QBD).

Failing To Provide An Evidentiary Specimen

Summary Offence
6 Months Imprisonment And / Or A Fine
Obligatory Disqualification

A person commits an offence if **both:**	
Step 1	**Step 2**
They **fail / refuse to provide a specimen** when required to do....	...and they **do not have a reasonable excuse** for failing to provide the specimen.

Exam Trip

- **No offence** of failure to provide an evidentiary specimen will be committed where a suspect:
    - ☐ Initially provided a specimen of breath of 50 micrograms or less (i.e. has not failed to provide);
    - ☐ Who subsequently elected to replace the specimen with urine or blood; and
    - ☐ Who later failed to provide the specimen of urine or blood.
- In such circumstances of a **refusal to provide the alternative blood or urine** – it is possible to **revert back to the breath specimen** for evidentiary purposes.

Exam Trip Up

- The provision of only **one specimen** of **breath** will result in the commission of the **offence** – (Remember 2 specimens are required – the higher of which will be disregarded).

Establishing A Reasonable Excuse

The **reasonable excuse** must emanate from **either**:			
Excuse 1	**Excuse 2**	**Excuse 3**	**Excuse 4**
Physical inability.	Mental inability.	Substantial risk to health.	Inability to understand – e.g. language barrier.

Arguments That Have Been Rejected By The Courts

The following arguments have been held **not** to amount to a **reasonable excuse** for failing to provide:				
Religious beliefs.	Refusal on legal advice.	Refusal to provide until a solicitor arrives to provide advice.	Refusal to provide until an appropriate adult arrives.	Self induced intoxication.

Taking Specimens From Those Incapable Of Providing Their Consent - Section 7(A) RTA 1988

Due to the procedural difficulties encountered where suspected **drivers are injured in accidents and are incapable of providing their consent to the taking of a sample** (e.g. because they are **unconscious**) **-** the following provisions now apply.

Step 1

A constable may make a request to a **medical practitioner** to take a specimen of **blood** from a person **without their consent** if it "**appears**" to the constable that **both:**	
Point 1	**Point 2**
The person has been involved in an **accident...**	...and the person is **incapable** of providing **consent** due to a **medical condition.**

Step 2

Once the **specimen has been obtained** the constable **must** (once the person is **conscious**):		
Task 1	**Task 2**	**Task 3**
Inform them that the specimen of blood was **taken.**	**Ask** them to provide their **permission** for the specimen to be used as an evidentiary specimen.	**Warn** them of the **consequences** of **refusal** - i.e. guilty of a **failure to provide**.

Step 3

If The Suspect Consents	If The Suspect Refuses
The specimen of blood is used in evidence.	The accused is guilty of failure to provide.

Who Will Be Permitted To Take The Specimen Whilst They Are Incapable Of Providing Their Consent

The medical practitioner who takes the specimen of blood:	
General Rule	**Exception To The General Rule**
Must be a **police medical practitioner unless** it is **not reasonably practicable.**	If a **non police medical practitioner** takes the specimen of blood – they must **not** be the practitioner **in charge of the suspect's clinical care.**

Hospital Procedure For Obtaining Evidentiary Samples – Obtaining The Authorisation Of A Medical Practitioner – Section 9 Road Traffic Act 1988

- An evidentiary sample cannot be obtained from a person in hospital without the **authorisation of the medical practitioner in immediate charge of their case.**
- They may refuse authorisation on the basis that it would be **prejudicial to the person's proper care and treatment.**

Detention Of Persons Following The Taking Of An Evidentiary Specimen - Section 10 Road Traffic Act 1988

A person who has been required to supply an evidentiary specimen of either breath, blood, or urine may **afterwards** **either**:	
Action 1	**Action 2**
Be **detained** at a police station	If the specimen was provided away from a police station – be **arrested, taken to** and **detained** at a **police station**
...if a constable had reasonable grounds for **believing** that, were the person to either **drive** or **attempt to drive** a mechanically propelled vehicle **(MPV)** on a **road,** they would **commit an offence** under **either** **section 4 or section 5.**	

Exam Trip Up

- If the belief was established in relation to a person from whom the evidentiary sample was taken at a **hospital** – they can only be arrested and taken to the police station if doing so would **not prejudice their proper care and treatment.**

Road Policing
Subject 3: Protection of Drivers & Passengers (Formerly Safety Measures)

A – Seat Belt Offences - Persons Aged 14 Or Over

Section 14(3) RTA 1988
Summary Only Offences
Penalty In The Magistrates Court – Fine Only

It is an offence for a person **aged 14 or over** to either:		
Action 1	**Action 2**	**Action 3**
Drive a **motor vehicle**	**Ride** as a **front passenger** of a **motor vehicle**	**Ride** in the **rear seat** of a **motor car** or a **passenger car**
...without wearing an adult seatbelt.		

Exam Trip Up

- The **driver** of the vehicle will **not** be held **criminally responsible** for any passenger not wearing a seat belt – i.e. there is **no offence of aiding and abetting**. - **only** the person **not wearing** the **seatbelt** will be **guilty**.
- For example: A driver wearing a belt who allows a passenger in his car who is not wearing a belt will not be guilty of the offence. Only the non belt wearing passenger will be guilty.
- Note how the section 14(3) offence relating to passengers 14 or over differs to that of section 15 offence which relates to passengers under 14 who are not wearing a seatbelt.
- Under section 15:
  - The driver who is wearing a seatbelt will be guilty in relation to the failure of the child under 14 to wear a seatbelt; and
  - The child under 14 will technically be guilty of aiding and abetting the offence.

Who Is Exempt From Wearing A Seatbelt? - Medical Certificates – Section 14(4) Road Traffic Act 1988

A person will be exempt if they possess a **medical certificate signed by a doctor** stating **both**:	
Point 1	**Point 2**
That the wearing of a seatbelt is **inadvisable** on **medical grounds**	The **duration** of the certification
...and a constable may **request the certificate to be produced either**:	
On request.	To a **police station** within **7 days**.

Delivery Drivers & Their Passengers – Section 14(2)(b)(i) Road Traffic Act 1988

Both the:	
Driver	Any **passenger**
...of a **motor vehicle** which has been **either**:	
Constructed for **carrying goods**	**Adapted** for **carrying goods**
...will be **exempt** if they travel without a seatbelt on journeys of **50 meters or less** with the **purpose** of **either**:	
Delivering anything.	**Collecting** anything.

Exam Trip Up

- Watch out for questions involving a delivery driver or passenger not wearing a seatbelt whilst carrying out a delivery in a **family car** - as the vehicle will **not** have been **constructed** or **adapted** for carrying goods they will **not be exempt.**

Exam Trip Up

- Watch out for questions involving a delivery driver or passenger not wearing a seatbelt in a vehicle which has been **constructed** or **adapted** for carrying goods but the **purpose** of the journey is **not to deliver or collect anything** - they will **not be exempt.**

B - Seat Belt Offences For Persons Under 14

Section 15(1) RTA 1988
Summary Only Offences
Penalty In The Magistrates Court – Fine Only

A person must **not without reasonable excuse** drive a **motor vehicle** on the **road** where **either**:

Situation 1	Situation 2	Situation 3	Situation 4
■ A child under the age of 14 is sitting in the front seat; and ■ They are not wearing a seatbelt.	Either: ■ A child under the age of 3 is in a rear seat; or ■ A child aged 3 or over but under 14 is in the rear seat and a belt is fitted; and They are not wearing a seatbelt.	A child who is: ■ Under 12; ■ Under 150cm; Is in the rear of a passenger car; and No belt is fitted in the rear; and The front seat has a belt; and Nobody is sitting in the front seat.	A child who is: ■ In the front of a motor vehicle (not a bus); ■ In a rear facing child restraining device; and The passenger seat is protected by an airbag; Unless the airbag is deactivated.

Who Is Guilty?

- It is the actual **driver** who is **guilty** of the offence – **not** the **person under 14.**

Airbag Deactivation?

- There is **no requirement** for either **front or side airbag** to be **deactivated** when a **child is sat facing the front.**

Suitable Seatbelts

Category	**Small Child**	**Large Child**	**Person Aged 14 Or Above**
Definition	Under 12 & Less than 135 cm tall	Under 14 & Not a small child	Self explanatory
Seatbelt That Must Be Worn	A child restraint appropriate for their height and weight.	Either: ■ A child restraint appropriate for their height and weight; or ■ Adult belt.	Must wear an adult belt

C – Riding A Motorcycle Without Protective Headgear

Section 16 RTA 1988
Summary Only Offence
Penalty In The Magistrates Court – Fine Only

<table>
<tr><td colspan="2">It is an offence to <u>either</u>:</td></tr>
<tr><td>Drive</td><td>Ride on (i.e. pillion passenger)</td></tr>
<tr><td colspan="2">...a motor <u>bi</u>cycle (i.e. 2 wheels) without a (BS standard or equivalent) helmet.</td></tr>
</table>

Drive

- A person will **not** commit an offence if they are only **pushing** the motor bicycle along whilst walking alongside it.
- An offence will be committed if they are **straddling** the motor bicycle and **propelling it with their feet** (even if the engine is switched off) – Crank v Brooks [1980] RTR 441.

Ride On

- **Riding on** relates to **pillion passengers.**

Exam Trip Up – Sidecar Passengers

- **Sidecar passengers** are **not required** to wear a helmet.

Exam Trip Up

- The **engine does not need to be switched on** – the propulsion of the motor bicycle can come from human force.

Motor Bicycle

- The offence only relates to motorised cycles with **2 wheels.**

Exam Trip Up

- Watch out for questions involving persons riding either a motorised **tricycle** or **quad bike** without a helmet – no offence will be committed as the vehicles have **more than 2 wheels**.

Exam Trip Up

- Watch out for questions involving persons riding a **motor bicycle** with a **sidecar** attached without a helmet – the **wheels on the sidecar will not count** and as the **bicycle has 2 wheels** the offence will be committed.

Without A Helmet

The **helmet** must **either**:	
Option 1	**Option 2**
Be **BS standard marked**.	If it is not BS standard marked – provide **as good or greater protection** than a BS standard marked helmet.

Exam Trip Up – Improperly Fastened Helmets

A person will be treated as without a helmet if they are **actually wearing a helmet but** it is **either**:	
Unfastened.	**Improperly fastened.**

Exemptions

The following are **exempt**:	
Exemption 1	**Exemption 2**
Sikhs who are wearing a **turban** at the time of driving or riding on the motor bicycle.	**Motor mowers.**

Who Is Guilty Of The Offence If There Are Un-Helmeted Passengers? – Section 16(4) RTA 1988

The General Rule **Passenger 16 Or Over**	**The Exception To The General Rule** **Passenger Under 16**
Only the person **failing to wear the helmet** is guilty. For example: ■ A helmeted driver will not be responsible for an un-helmeted passenger. ■ Only the un-helmeted passenger will be guilty in such circumstances.	If the **passenger** is **under 16** - **both** of the following will be guilty: ■ **Helmeted driver;** and ■ **Un-helmeted passenger.**

D - Passengers on Motorcycles

Section 23 RTA 1988
Summary Only Offence
Penalty In The Magistrates Court – Fine Plus Discretionary Disqualification

How Many Passengers May Be Carried?

- Only **1 passenger** may be carried on a motor bicycle – if more than 1 passenger is carried an offence will be committed.

How Must The 1 Passenger Be Carried?

An offence will be committed if the way in which the **1 passenger** is carried does **not satisfy all of the following criteria** – they must be:		
Step 1	**Step 2**	**Step 3**
Sitting **astride** the motor bicycle. – i.e. not side-saddle.	On a **proper seat** which is **securely fixed**.	**Behind** the driver's seat.

Who Will Be Guilty Of The Offence?

- Even though it is the passenger who is improperly carried - the **driver** will **commit the offence**.
- The **passenger** can be convicted of **aiding and abetting**.

E – Speed Limits - Restricted Roads – 30 MPH – Section 81(1) Road Traffic Regulation Act 1984

A restricted road (which has a 30 mph speed limit) will be established where:	
Situation 1	**Situation 2**
The road lamps are **not more than 200 yards apart.** If so – it is **not necessary for road signs** stating the limit to be placed. NB - the **traffic authority** has the **power** to **un-restrict** the road (by placing signs).	The road lamps are **more than 200 meters apart** but the traffic authority has expressly **directed that it is restricted.** If so – **road signs** stating the limit **must be placed**.

Exemptions From Speed Limits For Police, Fire & Ambulance Services

Speed limits shall not apply to **any vehicle** used for the **purposes** of any of the following **services:**			
Police	**SOCA**	**Fire**	**Ambulance**
...provided the driver **<u>either</u>**:			

Exemption 1	**Exemption 2**
Has previously **completed their training** in high speed driving.	Is **undergoing training** as a high speed driver at the time of speeding.

Exam Trip Up

- The vehicle does not need to be owned by any of the services – provided **<u>any vehicle</u>** is driven for the **purposes of the service** it will be exempt.
- Therefore a privately owned vehicle driven for the purposes of one of the services would also be exempt.

Exam Trip Up

- At the time of speeding the driver must be **performing the functions of the service**.
- Watch out for questions where the driver is speeding in a service vehicle and is off duty or is carrying out a personal errand unrelated to their duties.

Proof Of Speeding – The Need For Corroboration

A person **canno**t be **convicted** of speeding on the evidence of **1 witness alone** – there must be **corroboration** which can come from **either**:

Option 1	Option 2	Option 3
Speed measuring equipment in **police vehicles**.	**Vascar** speed measuring equipment. Nicholas v Penny [1950] 2 All ER 89	**2 police officers.** NB – they must **both see** the vehicle **speeding** at **exactly the same time.** *Brighty v Pearson* [1938] 4 All ER 127

Exam Trip Up

- While it may be preferable, it is not necessary to prove the accuracy of the equipment being used - *Darby v DPP* [1995] RTR 294.

What Is The Maximum Duration That Traffic Authorities Can Impose Temporary Speed Restrictions Due To Road Works etc?

- The restrictions **cannot generally exceed 18 months without approval** from the **Secretary of State.**

Traffic Calming

- The Road Traffic Regulation Act 1984 (Amendment) Order 1999 (SI 1999/1608) allows **local traffic authorities** the power to create **20 mph zones.**

Road Policing
Subject 4: Highways & Safety Measures (Formerly Other Measures Affecting Safety)

A – Highways & Safety

Obstructing The Highway, Obstructing A Road & Obstructing A Street

Obstructing The Highway	**Obstructing A Road**	**Obstructing A Street**
Section 137 Highways Act 1980	**Regulation 103 Road Vehicles (Construction And Use) Regulations 1986**	**Section 28 Town Polices Clauses Act 1847**
An offence is committed by any person who: ☐ **Without lawful:** ■ **Authority**; or ■ **Excuse;** ☐ **Wilfully obstructs a highway.**	■ An offence is committed by any **person in charge** of either: ☐ A **motor vehicle**; or ☐ **Trailer;** ■ Who either: ☐ **Causes;** or ☐ **Permits;** ■ It to **stand on a road;** ■ So as to cause an **unnecessary obstruction of the road.**	An offence is committed by any person in any **street** who: ☐ To the **obstruction, annoyance** or **danger** of either: ■ **Residents;** or ■ **Passengers;** ☐ Either: ■ **Wilfully interrupts** any **public crossing**; or ■ Causes any **wilful obstruction** in any **public footpath.**
Summary Only Offence: Penalty In The Magistrates Court – Fine Only	Summary Only Offence: Penalty In The Magistrates Court – Fine Only	Summary Only Offence: Penalty In The Magistrates Court – 14 Days Imprisonment And / Or A Fine

B – Causing A Danger

Causing A Danger To Other Road Users

Section 22A Road Traffic Act 1988
Either Way Offence
Penalty In The Crown Court – 7 Years Imprisonment And Or A Fine
Penalty In The Magistrates Court – 6 Months Imprisonment And Or A Fine

<table>
<tr><td colspan="6">A person commits an offence if they intentionally and without <u>either</u>:</td></tr>
<tr><td colspan="3">Lawful authority</td><td colspan="3">Reasonable excuse</td></tr>
<tr><td colspan="6"><u>Either</u>:</td></tr>
<tr><td colspan="2">Cause anything to be on or over the road</td><td colspan="2">Interfere with a motor vehicle, trailer or cycle</td><td colspan="2">Interfere directly or indirectly with traffic equipment</td></tr>
<tr><td colspan="6">...in such circumstances as it would be obvious to a reasonable person that to do so would be dangerous.

NB – An objective test – the accused need not have foreseen or intended the creation of a danger.</td></tr>
</table>

Dangerous Activities On A Highway

Summary Offences
Penalty In The Magistrates Court – Fine

Section 161 Highways Act 1980

A person commits an offence if they **without either**:				
Lawful authority		**Reasonable excuse**		
Either:				
Action 1	**Action 2**	**Action 3**	**Action 4**	**Action 5**
Deposits anything on the highway – and as a consequence a user of the highway is either: ■ Injured; or ■ Endangered.	Lights a fire on or over the highway...and as a consequence a user of the highway is either: ■ Injured; ■ Interrupted; or ■ Endangered.	Discharges a firearm or firework within 50 feet of the centre of the highway...and as a consequence a user of the highway is either: ■ Injured; ■ Interrupted; or ■ Endangered.	Allows any of the following to run or flow onto the highway from an adjoining premises: ■ Filth; ■ Dirt; ■ Lime; or ■ Other offensive matter.	Plays either football or another game on the highway to the annoyance of a user of the highway.

Section 161A Highways Act 1980

A person commits an offence if they **either**:		
Action 1	**Action 2**	
Light a fire on any land not forming part of the highway	**Directs** or **permits** a **fire to be lit** on any land not forming part of the highway	
...and the **smoke** from the fire causes the **result** of a user of the highway suffering either:		
Endangerment.	**Injury.**	**Interruption.**

Section 162 Highways Act

A person commits an offence if they place <u>**either**</u>:		
A **rope**	A **wire**	Any other **apparatus**
...**across a highway** in such manner as to **cause a danger** to **persons on a highway** – **unless** they can prove that they had **taken all necessary means to give adequate warning of the danger**.		

C - Parking

Parking Of Heavy Commercial Vehicles On Verges

Section 19 Road Traffic Act 1988
Summary Only Offence
Penalty In The Magistrates Court – Fine Only

It is an offence to **park** a **heavy commercial vehicle (over 7.5 tonnes) wholly** or **partly** <u>**either**</u>:				
On the **verge** of a road	**Between carriageways**	On a **footway**		
...**unless** it was **parked** <u>**either**</u>:				
With the **permission of a constable in uniform.**	For the **purpose** of either: ☐ **Saving life;** ☐ **Putting out fire;** ☐ **An emergency.**	It was there for **unloading.**	It could **not otherwise** have been unloaded.	It was **never unattended.**

Leaving A Vehicle In A Dangerous Position

Summary Only Offence
Penalty In The Magistrates Court – Fine Plus Discretionary Disqualification

<table>
<tr><td colspan="6">An offence is committed by a person in charge of a vehicle or trailer who <u>either</u>:</td></tr>
<tr><td colspan="3">Causes</td><td colspan="3">Permits</td></tr>
<tr><td colspan="6">...it to remain at rest on a road in <u>either</u>:</td></tr>
<tr><td colspan="2">Such a position</td><td colspan="2">Such condition</td><td colspan="2">Such circumstances</td></tr>
<tr><td colspan="6">...as to involve a danger of injury to other road users.</td></tr>
</table>

Abandoning Motor Vehicles

Section 2(1) Refuse Disposal (Amenity) Act 1978
Summary Only Offence
Penalty In The Magistrates Court – Fine Only

<table>
<tr><td colspan="2">An offence is committed by any person who without lawful authority <u>either</u>:</td></tr>
<tr><td>Situation 1</td><td>Situation 2</td></tr>
<tr><td>Abandons on any land in the open air or any highway either:
■ A motor vehicle; or
■ Anything which formed part of a motor vehicle and was removed from it whilst dismantling the vehicle on land.</td><td>Abandons on any land in the open air or any highway anything (i.e. - not a motor vehicle) brought there for the purpose of abandoning it.</td></tr>
</table>

Exam Trip Up

- Disposing of **vehicles, trailers or anything forming part thereof** would be included.
- The definition also includes **'anything'** other than the aforementioned items of property and would therefore include **private property, providing it is in the open air.**

D – Removal

Removal Of Abandoned Motor Vehicles – Section 3 Refuse Disposal (Amenity) Act 1978

The **local authority** has a **duty to remove** any **motor vehicle abandoned without lawful authority** on **either**:	
Location 1	**Location 2**
Any **land in the open air.**	Any **highway.**

Police Powers To Remove Vehicles From The Road – Regulation 3 Removal And Disposal Of Vehicles Regulations 1986

<table>
<tr><td colspan="3">A constable may require <u>either</u>:</td></tr>
<tr><td>The owner of a vehicle</td><td>The driver of a vehicle</td><td>The person either in charge or control of a vehicle</td></tr>
<tr><td colspan="3">...which has <u>either</u>:</td></tr>
<tr><td>Broken down on a road</td><td colspan="2">Been permitted to remain at rest on a road</td></tr>
<tr><td colspan="3">...to remove the vehicle <u>either</u>:</td></tr>
<tr><td>To a road</td><td colspan="2">Off the road</td></tr>
<tr><td colspan="3">...if it is <u>either</u>:</td></tr>
<tr><td>In a position or condition likely to cause obstruction or danger.</td><td colspan="2">In contravention of a restriction or prohibition.</td></tr>
</table>

Removal Of Parked Vehicles

Regulation 4 Removal And Disposal Of Vehicles Regulations 1986

<table>
<tr><td colspan="6">Where a vehicle is permitted to remain at rest on a road <u>either</u>:</td></tr>
<tr><td colspan="2">In contravention of a prohibition or restriction</td><td colspan="2">In a position or circumstances that will obstruct or cause danger</td><td colspan="2">On any land in open air and appears to have either been:
■ Abandoned; or
■ Broken down;</td></tr>
<tr><td colspan="6">...a constable may arrange for it to be <u>removed</u> from that road to another position <u>either</u>:</td></tr>
<tr><td colspan="3">On that road.</td><td colspan="3">On another road.</td></tr>
</table>

E – Clamping Vehicles On Private Land

- If an owner of private land displays a clear notice informing persons that vehicles parking without authority may be clamped – any driver who subsequently parks will be deemed to have "consented" to the clamping.
- Any attempts by the owner of the vehicle to remove a clamp in such circumstances which causes damage to the clamp will be guilty of criminal damage – *Lloyd v DPP* [1991] Crim LR 904.

F – Contravention Of A Traffic Regulation Order

Section 5(1) Road Traffic Regulation Act 1984
Summary Offence
Penalty In The Magistrates Court - Fine

An offence will be committed by a person who **either**:		
Contravenes a **road traffic order**	**Uses** a **vehicle** to **contravene** a **road traffic order**	**Causes** or **permits** a **vehicle** to be **used** to **contravene** a **road traffic order**
...**unless** the person is entitled to a **disabled persons concession** and had **displayed a recognised badge.**		

G – Tampering And Getting Onto Motor Vehicles

Tampering With Motor Vehicles

Section 25 Road Traffic Act 1988
Summary Only Offence
Penalty In The Magistrates Court – Fine Only

A person will commit an offence if in relation to a **motor vehicle** on **either** a:	
Road	**Local authority parking place**
...they **either**:	
Get onto the vehicle	**Tamper** with the **brakes** or other **mechanism**
...without either a:	
Lawful authority.	**Reasonable excuse.**

Exam Trip Up

- This offence can only be committed on the **road** or in a **Public Authority car park** - no other type of car park will do.

Exam Trip Up

- The offence only relates to **motor vehicles** - the offence cannot be committed against a trailer.

Holding Onto A Vehicle In Motion

Section 26 RTA 1988
Summary Only Offence
Penalty In The Magistrates Court – Fine Only

A person commits an offence if for the **purpose of being carried** - they **without either**:	
Lawful authority	**Reasonable excuse**
...either:	
Take hold of	**Get onto**
...either a:	
A **motor vehicle**	A **trailer**
...which is **in motion** on a **road.**	

Memory Tip

- An easy way to separate the finer points of the offence under section.25 (Tampering) with the offence under section 26 (holding or getting on to a vehicle in motion) is that:
  - ☐ The **section 25** offence does **not involve trailers** and must be committed on a **road or parking place provided by a local authority;**
  - ☐ Whereas the **section 26** offence involves **trailers** and must take place on a **road.**

H – Wrongful Use Of A Disabled Person's Badge

Section 117 Road Traffic Regulations Act 1984
Summary Offence
Penalty In The Magistrates Court - Fine

An offence will be committed where a person **both:**	
Displays on their vehicle a **blue disabled badge**	**Uses it** in circumstances where a **disabled person's concession** would be **available**
...**unless** the **badge** was **both:**	
Properly displayed.	**Properly issued to them.**

I – Off Road Driving

Summary Only Offence
Penalty In The Magistrates Court – Fine Only

A person commits an offence if they **without lawful authority drive** a **mechanically propelled vehicle (MPV)** on either:	
Any **common land, moorland** or any **land not forming part of a road**	On any **road** being a **footpath, bridleway,** or **restricted byway**
...**unless** they drive the **MPV** on any **land within 15 yards of a road** (upon which a vehicle may lawfully be driven) for the **purpose of parking** the vehicle on the land, or is driven there to **save life** or **extinguish a fire**.	

J – Builder's Skips

Summary Only Offence
Penalty In The Magistrates Court – Fine Only

Obtaining Permission To Deposit A Skip - Section 139(1) Highways Act 1980

- A **skip** can only be **deposited** with the **written permission** of the **Highways Authority.**

When Will An Offence Be Committed? - Section 139(4) Highways Act 1980

The **owner** of the skip and the **offender** will be guilty in the event of any of the following:				
Situation 1	**Situation 2**	**Situation 3**	**Situation 4**	**Situation 5**
Placing the skip **on a highway without permission.**	The skip **not** being **properly lit during darkness.**	The skip does **not bear** the **owners name** and **telephone number.**	The skip is **not removed as soon as possible after it is filled.**	There is a **failure to comply with any condition of the Highway Authority.**

Defence For The Owner Of The Skip - Section 139(6) Highways Act 1980

The **owner** may have a **defence** where <u>both</u>:	
Step 1	**Step 2**
The offence arose due to the **action** or **default of another...**	...and they had taken **all reasonable precautions** and **exercised due diligence to prevent the offence.**

Police Powers In Relation To Skips - Section 140(3) Highways Act 1980

- A **constable** in **uniform** may require the **removal of a skip in person** - failure to do so is an offence.

K - Road Works

Section 65(5) New Roads And Street Works Act 1991

Work sites must be properly:		
Guarded.	**Signed.**	**Lit.**

Removal Of Lighting Or Signs

It is an **offence to remove** any lighting or signs **without either**:	
Lawful authority.	**Reasonable excuse.**

L – Pedestrian Crossings

Exempt Persons Permitted To Cross Amber Or Red Lights

Regulations 12 & 13 Road Traffic Regulation Act 1984

<table>
<tr><td colspan="12">Any of the following groups will be permitted to cross an amber or red light at a crossing:</td></tr>
<tr><td colspan="3">Police</td><td colspan="3">Fire & Rescue</td><td colspan="3">Ambulance</td><td colspan="3">National Blood Service</td></tr>
<tr><td colspan="12">...provided <u>both</u>:</td></tr>
<tr><td colspan="6">Step 1</td><td colspan="6">Step 2</td></tr>
<tr><td colspan="6">The vehicle is being used for the purposes of the service</td><td colspan="6">Waiting at the light would hinder the purpose of the service</td></tr>
<tr><td colspan="12">...and <u>all</u> of the following criteria are also met:</td></tr>
<tr><td colspan="4">Step 3</td><td colspan="4">Step 4</td><td colspan="4">Step 5</td></tr>
<tr><td colspan="4">Precedence is accorded to any pedestrian on the carriageway.</td><td colspan="4">They do not proceed in a manner or time that is likely to endanger any person or vehicle at the crossing.</td><td colspan="4">They do not proceed in a manner or time that is likely to cause the driver of any vehicle at the crossing to change speed or course in order to avoid contact.</td></tr>
</table>

Exam Trip Up: School Crossings

- Section 28 of the Road Traffic Regulation Act 1984 has been amended by the Transport Act 2000 which **removed the former restrictions as to the time of day that an offence may be committed**, which were formerly the hours between 0800 hrs to 1730 hrs.

- Furthermore, school crossing patrols are no longer restricted to stopping traffic when children are crossing.

Road Policing
Subject 5: Accidents & Collisions

A – Reportable Accidents – Section 170 RTA 1988

<table>
<tr><td colspan="2">A reportable accident will arise when the presence of a mechanically propelled vehicle on <u>either</u>:</td></tr>
<tr><td>A road</td><td>A public place</td></tr>
<tr><td colspan="2">...causes an accident whereby <u>either</u>:</td></tr>
</table>

Consequence 1	**Injury** is caused to a **person other than the driver.**
Consequence 2	**Damage** is caused to **another vehicle.**
Consequence 3	**Damage** is caused to a **trailer drawn by an MPV.**
Consequence 4	**Damage** is caused to an animal (which is not inside that vehicle or trailer).
Consequence 5	**Damage** is caused to **property** that is either: ☐ **Constructed on;** ☐ **Fixed to;** ☐ **Growing on**; or ☐ **Forms part of**; .....either: ☐ The **road;** or ☐ **Areas adjacent** to the road.

Where Must The Accident Take Place?

- The accident must occur on either a **road** or **public place**.

Exam Trip Up

- An accident on **private land** will **not be reportable.**

Consequence 1 – Learning Points

Who Must Be Injured By The MPV?

An accident **will be reportable** if **either** of the following are **injured:**	
A **passenger** in the **MPV** was **injured.**	**Any other person outside of the MPV.**

Exam Trip Up

- An accident will **not** be **reportable** if the only person **injured** is the **driver** of the **MPV.**

Injury

Injury will include **both:**	
Physical injury.	**Psychological** injury (including shock).

Consequence 2 – Learning Points

Damage To Another Vehicle

- It will only be necessary to report an accident concerning damage to a vehicle where **another vehicle has been damaged by the MPV.**

Exam Trip Up

- The accident will **not** be **reportable** if the **only damage** was caused to the **MPV itself**.

Exam Trip Up - Which Form Of Vehicle Can Be Damaged?

- Any form of **vehicle** may be damaged by the MVP - the vehicle damaged **does not also need not be an MPV** (although it could be).

Consequence 3 – Learning Point

Which Trailer Can Be Damaged?

The **trailer** damaged can be **attached** to either:	
The driver's **own MPV.**	**Another vehicle.**

Consequence 4 – Learning Points

Definition Of An Animal – Section 170(8) RTA 1988

An **animal** will include any:					
C	**H**	**A**	**M**	**P**	**S**
Cattle	Horse	Ass	Mule	Pig	Sheep
D			**G**		
Dog			Goat		

Exam Trip Up

- The definition of animal - does **not** include **cats**.

Exam Trip Up

- An accident will **not** be **reportable** if the animal is either in the driver's **own MPV** or the driver's **own trailer.**

Exam Trip Up – What Action Must Be Taken If The Accident Occurred When The Driver Was Not In The Vehicle?

- The case of *Cawthorn v DPP* [2000] RTR 45 established that a driver will still be **obliged to report an accident even when they were not in the vehicle at the time of the accident** - e.g. the driver leaves the vehicle to pop a letter in a post box and the car runs off down a hill, crashing into a wall.

Exam Trip Up – What Action Must Be Taken If The Driver Was Not At Fault?

- The **duty to report** will **still arise** even if the driver is **not at fault** in causing the accident – *Harding v Price* [1948] 1 All ER 283.

What If The Driver Claims To Be Unaware That The Accident Has Taken Place?

- A driver will **not have to report** an accident if they are **unaware** of its occurrence.

Proving A Lack Of Awareness By The Driver

Step 1	Step 2
The **prosecution** must **initially prove** that an **accident has occurred.**	Once it is proved that an accident has occurred – the **burden** then **shifts** onto the **defence** to prove on the **balance of probability** that they were **unaware of the occurrence of the accident.**

B – Driver's Responsibilities Following A Reportable Accident – Section 170(2) RTA 1988

The **driver** of the **MPV** must:		
Step 1 – Stop	**Step 2 – Provide Details**	**Step 3 - Report**
Stop And...	**If required** by any **person having reasonable grounds** for doing so - **provide:** ■ The **driver's name** and **address;** ■ The **name** and **address** of the **owner** of the vehicle; ■ The **identification mark** of the vehicle.	Or... If the driver **does not give their name and address** - they must ASAP **report** the accident to **either:** ■ A police officer; or ■ A police station.

For How Long Must The Driver Stop?

- The driver is only obliged to **stop and remain with their vehicle for such time as to allow interested individuals to request the driver's details**.
- The driver does **not need to make their own enquiries** to find such interested persons – *Mutton v Bates* [1984] RTR 256.

Exam Trip Up

- The case of *DPP v Bennett* [1993] RTR 175 established that it is **permissible to supply the address of your solicitor** when exchanging details.

C - Reporting The Accident - Section 170(3) RTA 1988

When the **driver does not provide their name and address** at the time of the accident - they must **report** the accident:	
As soon as possible	...and within a **maximum period of 24 hours**
...to **either**:	
A **police officer.**	At a **police station in person.**

Exam Trip Up

- Whilst there is a maximum prescribed period of 24 hours within which to report, this does not mean that the driver can leave reporting to the last minute when they have had ample opportunity to report the matter sooner. The driver must report the matter as **soon as is reasonably practicable** in the circumstances.

D – The Offences - Failing To Stop Or Report An Accident

Section 170(4) RTA 1988 - Summary Only Offence
Penalty In The Magistrates Court - 6 Months Imprisonment And / Or A Fine, Plus Discretionary Disqualification

A person commits an offence if following an accident they **either**:	
Consequence 1	**Consequence 2**
Fail to **stop.**	**Fail** to **report** the accident.

Exam Trip Up

- The court of Appeal in the case of *R v Clark* [2003] 2 Cr App R 23, held that a **failure** to either **stop** or **report** an accident would **not** however amount to the offence of **perverting the course of justice.** This is because the offence requires a **positive act** rather than an omission to act.

Obligation To Produce Insurance Documents – Section 170 RTA 1988

At The Time Of The Accident

At the time of the accident the driver shall **produce their insurance documentation** to **either**:	
A **constable.**	Any person having **reasonable grounds.**

After The Accident

- If they are **unable to do so at the time** of the accident the driver will have a **7 day period** to **produce** the documents **at a police station specified.**

- **Failure** to do so will be an **offence.**

Road Policing
Subject 6: Insurance

A – Requirement For Insurance

Contravening A Requirement For Insurance

Section 143(2) RTA 1988
Summary Only Offence
Penalty In The Magistrates Court - Fine, Plus Discretionary Disqualification

<table>
<tr><td colspan="2">It is an offence to <u>either</u>:</td></tr>
<tr><td>Use</td><td>■ Either:
☐ Cause; or
☐ Permit;
■ Another to use</td></tr>
<tr><td colspan="2">...a motor vehicle without insurance on <u>either</u> a:</td></tr>
<tr><td>Road.</td><td>Public place.</td></tr>
</table>

Exam Trip Up

- Generally, the offence under section143 of one of **absolute liability**, in that you need not prove any intent or guilty knowledge by the defendant in order to convict - *Tapsell v Maslen* [1967] Crim LR 53.
- If however, a person allows another to use their vehicle on the express condition that the other person insures it first, the lender cannot be convicted of 'permitting' - *Newbury v Davis* [1974] RTR 367.

Defence – Section 143(3) RTA 1988

A driver with no insurance will have a **defence** when <u>**either**</u>:		
Defence 1	**Defence 2**	**Defence 3**
The vehicle did **not belong to them** and was **not** in their possession **under a contract of hire or loan.**	They were using the vehicle **during the course of their employment.**	They **neither knew** nor had reason to **believe** that there was **no insurance.**

Factors That Do Not Render A Policy Of Insurance Void – Section 148(2)(a) – (h) RTA 1988

Breach of the following does **not make the policy of insurance void**:	
☐ The driver's age or mental condition; ☐ The vehicle's condition; ☐ The number of persons carried in the vehicle; ☐ The weight or characteristics of goods carried;	☐ The times or areas in which the vehicle is used; ☐ The power or value of the vehicle; ☐ Carrying any apparatus or any identification of the vehicle.

Registered Keeper Of An Uninsured Vehicle – Section 144A RTA 1988

- If a **motor vehicle registered** under the Vehicle Excise and Registration Act 1994 **does not meet** the **insurance requirements** – the **person in whose name the vehicle is registered** is guilty of an **offence.**

When Will A Vehicle Meet Insurance Requirements?

Step 1	The vehicle is covered by a policy of insurance or such security in respect of 3rd party risk....and...

Step 2	Either: ■ The policy or security, or the certificate of insurance or security which relates to it, identifies the vehicle by its registration mark as a vehicle which is covered by the policy or security; or ■ The vehicle is covered by the policy or security because the policy or security covers any vehicle, or any vehicle of a particular description, the owner of which is a person named in the policy or security or in the certificate of insurance or security which relates to it & the vehicle is owned by that person.

B - Power To Demand Production Of Insurance Documents – Section 165(1) – (5) RTA 1988

<table>
<tr><td colspan="3"><u>Either</u> a:</td></tr>
<tr><td colspan="2">Constable</td><td>Vehicle examiner</td></tr>
<tr><td colspan="3">Can request that <u>any</u> of the following persons:</td></tr>
<tr><td>Person 1</td><td>Person 2</td><td>Person 3</td></tr>
<tr><td>A person driving a motor vehicle on a road</td><td>A person whom they reasonably believe to have been the driver when an accident occurred owing to their presence on a road or public place</td><td>A person who they reasonably believe to have committed an offence in relation to the use of the vehicle on the road</td></tr>
<tr><td colspan="3">...to provide all of the following:</td></tr>
<tr><td>Point 1</td><td>Point 2</td><td>Point 3</td></tr>
<tr><td>Their name and address.</td><td>The name and address of the vehicle owner.</td><td>The certificate of insurance of that vehicle (and any test certificate).</td></tr>
<tr><td colspan="3">...and a failure to do so is an offence.</td></tr>
</table>

Defence - Insurance Documents Not Produced At The Time Of the Request -Section 165(4)(a) – (c) RTA 1988

A **driver who does not produce their insurance documents at the time of the request** will have a **defence** provided <u>**either**</u>:

Defence 1	Defence 2	Defence 3
Their insurance documents are **produced within 7 days** at a specified police station.	Their insurance documents are **produced as soon as was reasonably practicable.**	It was **not practicable to produce the insurance documents before the proceedings began.**

Vehicles Being Towed?

- When motor vehicles are being **towed** by other vehicles, they **remain 'motor vehicles'.**
- It is **irrelevant** whether the vehicle's **ignition was switched on or off** - there would still be a requirement for insurance.

The Road Traffic Act 1988 (Retention and Disposal of Seized Motor Vehicles) Regulations 2005 (SI 2005/1606)

- Underline the procedures which the police must adhere to, after utilising the power of seizure for vehicles with no insurance.

Seizure Notice	Authentication
The vehicle **owner** or **keeper** must be given a **seizure notice,** which gives specific information regarding the seizure and retention of the vehicle in question. Details will include: ■ A warning that any appropriate **charges must be paid;** ■ The person collecting the vehicle at the material time must **produce a valid driver's licence** and **confirmation of insurance** covering such use of the vehicle, at a **police station** or **in person to a police officer**; or ■ They can **nominate a third person** who can produce those documents in respect of that person's use of the vehicle to whom the vehicle can be released) (Reg. 4(3)–(4)).	The person claiming the vehicle can: ■ **Authenticate** that they are the **vehicle's owner;** and ■ **Pay the release / seizure fee**; or ■ **Nominate a third person** who provides evidence of a valid insurance certificate and driver's license covering their use of the vehicle. In these circumstances, the **authorised person (owner) must permit the third person to remove the vehicle**. (Reg. 5(2).

Exam Trip Up

A **nominated person** *may* **recover the vehicle** and also **produce the documents** at a police station or to a police constable (Reg. 4) and later at the place where the vehicle is being held (reg. 5).

Exempt Vehicles - Section 144 Road Traffic Act 1988

- The occasions whereby vehicles will be **exempt** from requiring a **policy of insurance** include:
    - ☐ **Police authority vehicles;** and
    - ☐ **Vehicles being used for police purposes.**
- The case of *Jones v Chief Constable of Bedfordshire* [1987] RTR 332, found that this will **include occasions when an off-duty police officer uses their own vehicle for police purposes.**

Exam Trip Up

- In the case of *Ballance* v *Brown* [1955] Crim LR 384, it was decided that taking a **2 mile detour to give someone a lift,** does **not make the employers insurance invalid**.
- In the case of *Marsh* v *Moores* [1949] 2 All ER 27, it was deemed that an **employee driving a company vehicle for an unauthorised purpose will not invalidate the insurance.**

Road Policing
Subject 7: Construction & Use

A – The Road Vehicles (Construction & Use) Regulations 1986

Defective Tyres

Regulation 27 Road Vehicles (Construction and Use) Regulations 1986

- A **tyre** is **defective** when:
  - It is **unsuitable for use**;
  - It is **under inflated** or **over inflated**;
  - It has a **cut** in **excess of 25mm** or **10% of its section width** (whichever is greater) and is deep enough to **reach the ply or cord**;
  - It has a **lump, bulge** or **tear** caused by failure of the structure;
  - **Ply** or **cord** is **exposed;**
  - It is **not maintained** in a condition **fit** for its use;
  - It has a **defect** that might cause **damage** to the **road** or to **persons;**
  - The **base of a groove in a tread is not visible**
  - Either:
    - The grooves of the **tread** of the tyre do **not have a depth** of at least **1 mm** throughout a **continuous band** measuring at least ¾ **of the breadth of the tread** round the entire **outer circumference**; or
    - If the grooves of the original tread did not extend beyond ¾ of the breadth of the tread, **any groove** which showed in the original tread does **not have a depth of** at least **1 mm.**

Brakes

Regulations 15 - 18 Road Vehicles (Construction and Use) Regulations 1986

Both of the following must be **maintained** in a good and efficient **working order:**	
Aspect 1	**Aspect 2**
Every part of every **braking system.**	The **means of operation** fitted to a vehicle.

Exam Trip Up

- It is not absolutely necessary for the person testing the braking system of a vehicle to be a 'qualified examiner'
- In the case of *Stoneley* v *Richardson* [1973] RTR 229 a constable testified to being able to push the defendant's car along with the handbrake applied - the evidence was accepted by the court.

Breach Of Brake Or Tyre Requirements – Section 41A RTA 1988

A person will commit an offence if they **either**:		
Situation 1	**Situation 2**	**Situation 3**
Fail to comply with regulations as to **breaks** or **tyres.**	**Uses on a road** a **motor vehicle** or **trailer** which does **not comply** with the regulations.	**Cause or permit another to use on a road** a **motor vehicle** or **trailer** which does **not comply** with the regulations.

Silencers

Regulations 54 and 57 Road Vehicles (Construction and Use) Regulations 1986

Every **vehicle propelled** by an **internal combustion engine:**	
Must be fitted with an **exhaust system** including a **silencer...**	...and the **exhaust gases** from the engine must not escape without **passing through** the **silencer**

Mirrors

Regulation 33 Road Vehicles (Construction and Use) Regulations 1986

With certain exceptions every:		
Passenger vehicle	**Goods** vehicle	**Dual purpose** vehicle
...first used on or **after 1st June 1978** must be equipped with all of the following:		
Factor 1	**Factor 2**	**Factor 3**
An **interior rear view mirror.**	At least one **exterior mirror** fitted to the **off side.**	If the **interior rear view mirror** is **obscured** the driver must have an **exterior rear view mirror** attached to the **near side** of the vehicle.

Quitting

Regulation 107 Road Vehicles (Construction and Use) Regulations 1986

It is an offence to **leave a motor vehicle unattended on a road unless** <u>**both**</u>:	
Criteria 1	**Criteria 2**
The **engine** has been **stopped.**	The **brake** has been **set.**

Exam Trip Up

- NB - **both must be done** - *Butterworth v Shorthouse* [1956] CRIM LR 341.

Attended?

- The person left **'attending'** the vehicle must be someone who is **licensed** to drive it and in a **position to intervene** - otherwise regulation 107 is breached.
- The person **does not have to be in the driver seat** or **any other seat** – they need only be **in a position to 'intervene'** which will be a **question of fact.**

Stopping Engines

Regulation 98 Road Vehicles (Construction and Use) Regulations 1986

The **driver** of a vehicle when **stationary** shall **stop** the action of any machinery attached to or forming part of the vehicle so far as is necessary to **prevent either**:	
Noise.	**Exhaust emissions.**

Exceptions Where Stationary Vehicles Are Permitted To Keep The Engine Running

Exceptions include situations where the vehicle is stationery due to **either**:			
Traffic.	The need to **examine machinery** following its **failure.**	The need to **work the vehicle** for a purpose **other than driving** the vehicle.	**Vehicles propelled by** gas produced **in plant** carried on the vehicle.

B – Offences

Using A Motor Vehicle In Dangerous Condition

Section 40A Road Traffic Act 1988
Summary Only Offence
Penalty In The Magistrates Court - Fine Plus Discretionary Disqualification

A person is guilty of an offence if they **either**:

Situation 1	Situation 2
Use themselves	☐ Either: ■ **Cause;** or ■ **Permit;** ☐ **Another** to **use**

...**either** a:

Motor vehicle	Trailer

..**on a road** when **any** of the following creates a **danger** to **any person:**

Danger 1	Danger 2	Danger 3	Danger 4	Danger 5	Danger 6
The **condition** of the: ■ Vehicle ■ Trailer ■ Accessories ■ Equipment.	The **purpose** for which it is used.	The **number** of **passengers** carried.	The **manner** in which **passengers** are carried.	The **weight, position** or **distribution** of its load.	The **manner** in which the **load** is **secured.**

Learning Point

- The existence of **danger** is a **question of fact** for the Magistrates or the jury.
- In the case of *DPP v Gray* [1999] RTR 339 - a young child was seen to be travelling in the open back of an uncovered jeep without any fitted restraints. The child was steadying himself by holding on to the vehicle's roll bars. The court held that, even though he had travelled in that way without incident on numerous previous occasions and that his father was generally a responsible parent, the objective test as to the potential for injury meant that the offence had been committed.

Exam Trip Up

- The offence does **not cover mechanically propelled vehicles.** The offence only applies to **motor vehicles.**

Breach Of Requirement: Brakes, Steering, Gear Or Tyres

Section 41A RTA 1988
Summary Only Offence
Penalty In The Magistrates Court – Fine

A person commits an offence if they either:		
Action 1	**Action 2**	**Action 3**
Contravene or **fail to comply** with a construction and use requirement as to breaks, steering, gear or tyres.	**Use on the road a motor vehicle** or **trailer** which does not comply with such a requirement.	**Cause** or **permit** a motor vehicle or trailer which does not comply with such a requirement to be used.

Breach Of Weights Requirements For Goods And Passenger Vehicles

Section 41B(1) RTA 1988
Summary Only Offence
Penalty In The Magistrates Court – Fine

A person will commit an offence if they **either**:		
Action 1	**Action 2**	**Action 3**
Fail to comply with the regulations in relation to **weights** applicable to: ■ A **goods vehicle;** ■ A **motor vehicle** or trailer adapted to carry **more than 8 passengers.**	**Use on a road** a vehicle that does not comply with the requirements.	**Cause or permit another to use on a road** a vehicle that does not comply with the requirements.

Defence - Section 41B(2) RTA 1988

It is a **defence** to prove that **either**:		
Defence 1	**Defence 2**	**Defence 3**
At the time the vehicle was being used on a road it was **proceeding to the nearest weighbridge to be weighed**	At the time the vehicle was being used on a road it was **proceeding from a weighbridge** to the **nearest point at which it was reasonably practicable to reduce the weight** to the relevant limit **without causing an obstruction** on the road.	If the vehicle was **not more than 5% overweight:** ■ The **limit was not exceeded at the original time of loading;** and ■ **No** person has **subsequently added the weight**.

C – Testing - Using, Causing or Permitting Use of Vehicle Without Test Certificate

Both Summary Offences
Penalty In The Magistrates Court – Fine Only

Using, Causing or Permitting Use of Vehicle Without Test Certificate **Section 47(1) Road Traffic Act 1988**	**Using, Causing Or Permitting Use Of Goods Vehicles Without Test Certificate** **Section 53(2) Road Traffic Act 1988**
A person commits an offence if they: ☐ Either: ■ **Use**; or ■ **Cause or permit** to be used; ☐ A **motor vehicle**; ☐ On a **road;** ☐ At **any time**; ☐ To which there is **no test certificate** been issued within the appropriate time (12 months or less as may be prescribed).	An offence will be committed by: ☐ Any person who at **any time after** the **relevant date**; ☐ Either ■ **Uses;** or ■ **Causes** or **permits** to be used; ☐ **On a road;** ☐ A **goods vehicle** of a **class required** to have submitted for a **goods vehicle test**; and; ☐ **At the time** of doing so there is **no test certificate in force.**

Exam Trip Up

- Vehicles **provided** (as opposed to **used**) for **police purposes** are **exempt** if they are **maintained** in an **approved workshop**.

Exam Trip Up

- An **exemption** exists where a person is **taking the motor vehicle either to or from a testing centre.**
- This only applies when the test has been **previously arranged** with the testing centre.

Supplying Unroadworthy Vehicles (Sec 75 Road Traffic Act 1988)

- In the case of *Devon County Council v DB Cars* [2002] Crim LR 71, it was held that where a **garage returned a vehicle to an owner, after stating that it had been repaired and had passed its MOT, when in fact it was unroadworthy,** the garage committed the offence of supplying an unroadworthy vehicle. In this case, the court held that '**supplying**' involved a **transfer of physical control** of an item from one person to another.

Vehicle Defect Rectification Scheme (VDRS)

- A **person issued with a defect form** must **submit the vehicle for examination** at a **Department for Transport approved testing station.**
- The testing station will **certify** that the **defect** has been **rectified** and will **endorse the form**.
- There is **no specific time limit within which this test must be conducted** - however, the **form itself must be submitted to the police station nominated within 14 days**, which effectively means that the vehicle must be examined within 14 days.

Road Policing
Subject 8: Driver Licensing & Forgery of Documents
Sergeants Syllabus Only

A - Driving Otherwise than in Accordance with Licence

Section 87 Road Traffic Act 1988
Summary Offence
Fine and Discretionary Disqualification Under Specified Circumstances

Is an offence for a person to <u>**either**</u>:	
Drive on a **road** a **motor vehicle** of any **class** otherwise than in accordance with a **licence authorising** him to drive a motor vehicle of **that class**.	**Cause or permit another person** to **drive** a **motor vehicle** of any **class** otherwise than in accordance with a **licence authorising** that other person to drive a motor vehicle of **that class.**

The Burden Of Proof

- Once the above offence is charged and the **prosecution** have **proved** that the **driving** was on a **public highway -** then it is up to the **defendant** to **prove** that he had the **relevant licence** and **insurance.**

Production Of Documentation

- There is **no obligation** on the **police** or any other **authority** to **serve any request for production** of the documentation – HORT/1.

- Also where, due to an accident which results in damage or injury, a vehicle is brought to a halt, the driver taken to hospital without exchanging details with others involved and later discharges himself from hospital without reporting details of the accident to the police, the driver has not satisfied the requirements to stop and exchange details and report the accident under the Road Traffic Act 1988.
  It makes no difference that the police observed the accident but made no request for information - *DPP v Hay* [2006] RTR 3.

  The offence stands when the defendant has driven without a licence or alternatively has breached a condition of a licence held.

Classes Of Vehicles That The Licence Authorises

- The **classes** of vehicles which the holder of a licence is **authorised** by that licence to drive are **stated on the licence itself** - a licence is valid only when used in accordance with its conditions of issue.

Exam Trip Up

- If an employer is told by their employee that they possess a full licence although in fact the employee only holds a provisional licence - if the employer allows the employee to drive their van without requiring to inspect the licence - the employer will not be guilty of aiding and abetting the employee to drive unlawfully, since the employer will not have deliberately shut their eyes to the fact.

- Where employers however ensured that their drivers had driving licences when they commenced employment but had no system to check that their employees renewed their licences, the employers were convicted under subsection 2 above.

B - Police Powers - Power To Demand Production Of Driving Licence – Section 164 Road Traffic Act 1988

Any of the following persons:				
A person **driving a motor vehicle on a road**	A person whom a constable or vehicle examiner has reasonable cause to **believe** to have **been the driver of a motor vehicle at a time when an accident occurred** owing to its presence on a road	A person whom a constable or vehicle examiner has reasonable cause to **believe** to have committed an **offence in relation to the use of a motor vehicle on a road**	A person who **supervises the holder of a provisional licence** while the holder is driving a motor vehicle on a road	A person whom a constable or vehicle examiner has reasonable cause to **believe was supervising a provisional licence holder while driving - at a time when an accident occurred** owing to the presence of the vehicle on a road or at a time when an offence is suspected of having been committed by the holder of the provisional licence in relation to the use of the vehicle on a road

....must, on being so **required** by a **constable or vehicle examiner** - **produce** their **licence** and its **counterpar**t for examination – to enable the person to ascertain the following information:

Fact 1	Fact 2	Fact 3
The **name** and **address** of the holder.	The **date of issue**.	The **authority** by which they were issued.

Exam Trip Up

- In short, the driver or person in charge of a motor vehicle on a road when a provisional licence holder is driving must **provide their licence** to an official **when requested** and the official must be allowed **time to examine** the said licence for their name and address, date and authority of issue.
- If the official has not had the required time to examine the document - then the requirement is not discharged.
- Unlike a certificate of insurance - driving licences must be produced **in person.**

Format Of The Licence

- The new Photo card Driving Licence consists of a credit card style licence showing an image of the holder and their signature.
- A paper counterpart Driving Licence is also issued giving details of the categories of vehicles a person can drive as a provisional licence holder, their entitlement history and any endorsements together with name and address and image of signature.

Failure To Provide A Driving Licence

- **Both parts** <u>**must**</u> be **produced** - it will be an offence under section 164(6) if only one part is produced.

Power To Demand A Date Of Birth – Section 164 Road Traffic Act 1988

A person required by a constable to produce his driving licence must also on being so required by the constable **state their date of birth** in the following prescribed circumstances:

Circumstance 1	Circumstance 2	Circumstance 3
Where the person **fails to produce the licence forthwith.**	Where the person produces a **licence** which the police constable has reason to **suspect** <u>**either:**</u> ☐ Was **not granted** to that person; ☐ Was granted to that person in **error;** ☐ Contains an **alteration to the particulars on the licence** other than the driver number, made with intent to deceive; or ☐ The **driver number has been altered, removed or defaced.**	Where the person is a **supervisor of a learner driver** and the police constable has reason to suspect that they are **less than 21 years of age**.

C - Driving While Disqualified

Section 103(1)(b) Road Traffic Act 1988
Summary Offence
Six Months Imprisonment And / Or A Fine & Discretionary Disqualification.

- A person is guilty of an offence if, while **disqualified** for holding or obtaining a licence they **drive a motor vehicle on a road.**

Exam Trip Up

- If a driver is disqualified and obtains a licence then that licence will have no effect.

Exam Trip Up

- In *Pinner v Everett* [1969] 1 WLR 1266 it was held that there was **no requirement for the vehicle to be in motion.**

Exam Trip Up

- If the driver is under age then they will not commit this offence.
- However the underage driver will commit the "driving otherwise than in accordance with their licence" offence contrary to section 87 (1) Road Traffic Act 1988.

Exam Trip Up

- The **prosecution must prove** that the driver of the motor vehicle was in fact **disqualified at the relevant time.**
- The court has accepted that evidence of a person present at the original court case where the driver was disqualified and admission of the driver both in interview and at court will be sufficient. *DPP v Mooney* [1997] RTR 434 & *Moran v CPS* [2000] 164 JP 562.

Exam Trip Up

- This offence is a summary offence and therefore cannot be attempted.

Exam Trip Up

- If a suspect denies being disqualified, a mere matching of details in the court register is insufficient - strict proof is required.

Exam Trip Up

- The same principle was applied to a memorandum of conviction if the defendant denies the convictions listed on it - *Bailey v DPP* [1998].

Exam Trip Up

If no suitable witness exists and the disqualification is being denied it may be difficult to find appropriate evidence - but the following may (or may not) **help to substantiate a court register extract**:		
Fingerprint evidence of the previous conviction may be available.	The officer in the original case could give identification evidence of the suspect and the circumstances of that offence.	If the suspect's driving licence records at the DVLA are available then they will show him as disqualified at the time of the original court hearing.

Exam Trip Up

- In the case of *DPP v Olakunori* [1998] - Olakunori denied a previous disqualification, but the prosecution used a combination of his birth certificate, passport and a number of lies he had told about his identity, along with the original court records, to satisfy magistrates as to Olakunori's identity.

Exam Trip Up

- The case of 'dock identifications' was covered in the case of *Barnes v DPP* [1997] 2 Cr App R 505. The court approved of some dock identifications at the discretion of Magistrates (not at the Crown Court) for lesser offences such as driving offences.
- In this case a police officer made a dock identification. They had performed an interview of Barnes at the scene of an accident. At the time identification was not an issue, but Barnes had given false details and subsequently tried to avoid conviction at the court hearing, so the officer was permitted to point him out in the dock.
- This should not be looked upon as a way to avoid formal identification procedures under Code D PACE1984 where they are normally required because of doubt over the identity of offender during the investigation.

D – Forgery - The Offences

Forgery Of Non Registration Documents

Section 173(1) RTA 1988
Either Way Offence
Penalty In The Crown Court – 2 Years Imprisonment And / Or A Fine
Penalty In The Magistrates Court – A Fine Only

An offence of **forgery** will be committed by any person who with the **intent** to **deceive** - **either**:		
Action 1	**Action 2**	**Action 3**
Forges, alters or **uses** a **relevant document** or **thing.**	**Lends,** or **allows another to use** a **relevant document** or **thing.**	**Makes** or **has in their possession** any **relevant document** or **thing** so closely **resembling** a relevant document or thing as to be **calculated to deceive.**

Definition Of A Relevant Document Or Thing - Section 173(2) RTA 1988

A **relevant document** or **thing** may include **either**:		
Licences	Insurance documents	Haulage permits
Test certificates	Certificates of exemption for seatbelts	Goods vehicles plates

Definition Of Forgery

- Forgery means making a false document in order that it may be used as genuine.

Exam Trip Up

- It is necessary to establish an intention to deceive.

Making False Statements Or Withholding Information – Section 174 RTA 1988

An offence will be committed by a person who **either**:	
Knowingly makes a **false statement** for the **purpose** of: ■ **Obtaining** a **licence;** ■ **Preventing** the **granting** of a **licence;** ■ **Procuring** a **provision** or **condition** on a **licence;** ■ **Obtaining** an **international road haulage permit**; or ■ **Securing** the **entry** or **retention** of the name of any person on the **register of approved instructors; or**	In **supplying information** or **producing documents** to achieve such an outcome either: ■ **Knowingly** or **recklessly** makes a **false statement;** ■ **Knowingly** or **recklessly** makes **use of a false document;** ■ **Knowingly produces a false statement** or **evidence** in a **declaration;** ■ **Wilfully** makes a **false record** in a **document required to be kept;** ■ With **intent** to deceive **makes use of a false record in a document required to be kept;** or ■ **Makes use of a false statement** or **withholds information** for the **purpose of the issue of insurance.**

- There is **no need** to prove that the person **gained** from their actions – *Ocean Accident etc Co. v Cole* [1932] 96 JP 191.

Police Powers In Relation To Documents Obtained Falsely or Forged Documents – Section 176 RTA 1988

A **constable** may **seize** a document if they have **reasonable cause** to **believe** that a document produced to them was **either**:	
Forged.	**Falsely obtained.**

Exam Trip Up

- Section 176 (4) of the Road Traffic Act 1988 provides a **power to seize** either a **document** or a **plate** from a vehicle where the constable reasonably **believes** that an offence under section 173 (forgery or falsification) has occurred.
- The **officer** removing the plate must be an **examiner appointed** under section 66A of the Act.
- This act and section does **not allow the officer to seize the vehicle**.

E – Other Offences Involving False Records & Forgery

Forgery Of Registration Documents

Sections 44 - 45 Vehicle Excise and Registration Act 1994
Either Way Offence
Penalty In The Crown Court – 2 Years Imprisonment And / Or A Fine
Penalty In The Magistrates Court – A Fine Only

A person will be guilty of an offence of **forging registration documents** if they carry out any of the following in respect of a vehicle registration document:

Action 1	Action 2	Action 3	Action 4
Forge it.	**Fraudulently alter it.**	**Fraudulently use it.**	**Lend** it or **allow another to use it** to do any of the above.

Forgery Of Documents Relating To PSV's

Section 65(2) Public Passenger Vehicles Act 1981
Either Way Offence
Penalty In The Crown Court – 2 Years Imprisonment
Penalty In The Magistrates Court – A Fine Only

An offence will be committed by any person who with **intent** to **deceive** - either:	
Action 1	**Action 2**
■ Either: ☐ **Forges;** ☐ **Alters;** ☐ **Uses;** ☐ **Lends** to another or **allows** another to **use;** ■ A **relevant document** or **thing**.	■ Either: ☐ **Makes;** or ☐ Has in their **possession;** ■ Any **document** or **thing** so **closely resembling** a **document** or **thing** as to be **calculated to deceive.**

Definition Of A Relevant Document Or Thing Relating To PSV's - Section 65(1) Public Passenger Vehicles Act 1981

A **relevant document** or **thing** may include any of the following:			
Document 1	**Document 2**	**Document 3**	**Document 4**
Licences.	**Certificates of fitness.**	**Certificates of type.**	**Operators disc certificates of competence.**

Forgery Relating To Goods Vehicles

Section 38 Goods Vehicles (Licensing Of Operators) Act 1995
Either Way Offence
Penalty In The Crown Court – 2 Years Imprisonment And / Or A Fine
Penalty In The Magistrates Court – A Fine Only

A person will be guilty of an offence if with **intent to deceive** they carry out any of the following in respect of a **document** or **thing** <u>**either**</u>:

Action 1	Action 2	Action 3	Action 4	Action 5
Forge it.	**Alter it.**	**Use it.**	**Lend it** or **allow it to be used.**	Have **in their possession** a **document** or **thing** so **closely resembling** a **document** or **thing** as to be **calculated to deceive.**

Misuse Of Parking Documents Or Apparatus

Section 115 Road Traffic Regulations Act 1984
Either Way Offence
Penalty In The Crown Court – 2 Years Imprisonment And / Or A Fine
Penalty In The Magistrates Court – A Fine Only

A person shall be guilty of an offence if with **intent to deceive** they <u>**either**</u>:

Use, lend or **allow** to be used: ■ Any **parking device** or **apparatus** designed to be used in connection with parking devices; ■ Any **ticket issued** by a **parking meter, parking device** or **apparatus;** ■ Any **authorisation** by a **certificate** or **other means of identification**; or ■ Any **permit or token.**	Either: ■ **Makes;** or ■ Has in their **possession;** ...anything **so closely resembling any such thing** as to be **calculated to deceive.**	**Knowingly** makes a **false statement** for the **purposes of procuring the grant or issue** or any such **authorisation.**

Road Policing
Subject 9: Notices Of Intended Prosecution - Sergeants Syllabus Only

A – Relevant Offences Requiring A Notice Of Intended Prosecution To Be Issued – Schedule 1 Road Traffic Offenders Act 1988

The following offences will **require a notice of intended prosecution** to be issued:				
Offence 1	**Offence 2**	**Offence 3**	**Offence 4**	**Offence 5**
Dangerous, careless, or inconsiderate driving.	Dangerous, careless, or inconsiderate cycling.	Leaving a vehicle in a dangerous position.	Failing to comply with traffic signs and directions.	Speeding offences under sections 16 and 17 of the Road Traffic Regulation Act 1984.

B - Exceptions Where It Will Not Be Necessary To Issue A Notice Of Intended Prosecution For Such Offences - Section 2(1) Road Traffic Offenders Act 1988

There is **no need to issue a notice of intended prosecution** for such offences if **either**:	
At the time of the act	**Immediately after the act**
...an **accident** occurred owing to the **presence** of the **vehicle** concerned **on a road.**	

Exam Trip Up

- It is **not necessary** for the **accident** to be **reportable** in nature.
- Any accident will suffice.

Exam Trip Up

- The accident must happen on a **road -** (NB – **public place** is **not included**).

Exam Trip Up – Drivers Unaware Of Minor Accidents

- If the **driver** is **unaware an accident has happened** because it is **so minor**, it **will be necessary to issue a notice of intended prosecution.**
- For example – In the case of *Bentley v Dickinson* [1983] RTR 356, a driver of a HGV was unaware they had clipped and damaged an object whilst going around a corner. In such circumstances it was necessary to issue a notice of intended prosecution.

Exam Trip Up – Drivers Who Cannot Remember An Accident Due To Its Severity

- The case of *DPP v Pidhajeckyj* [1991] RTR 136, established that where an **accident is so severe that the driver does not remember it happening,** it will **not** be **necessary to issue a notice of intended prosecution.**

C – Proof For Issuing Notices Of Intended Prosecution - Section 1 Road Traffic Offenders Act 1988

Prior to a defendant being **prosecuted** for **certain traffic offences** they must have **either**:

Option 1	Option 2	Option 3
Been **warned** of the possibility of **prosecution at the time of the offence.**	Been **served** with a **summons** or **charged within 14 days of the offence.**	**Received within 14 days of the offence** a **notice** setting out the possibility of prosecution. This will be sent to either: ■ The **driver** of the vehicle (e.g. a boy racer); or ■ The **registered keeper** of the vehicle (e.g. the parent who owns the car that the boy racer was using).

Who Will Issue The Warning Or Notice?

- The **warning** or **notice** must be **issued** by the **'prosecutor'** - this will normally be the **police.**

Exam Trip Up

- The case of *Swan v Vehicle Inspectorate* [1997] RTR 187 established that if the **person issuing** the warning is **not empowered** to make a decision whether or not to prosecute (e.g. a vehicle examiner) the **warning will be deemed not to have been issued**.

- The case of *Gibson v Dalton* [1980] RTR 410 established that if a ***verbal*** **notice of intended prosecution** is issued it is necessary to prove that the defendant **understood** the notice.

- As a result it will be common practice to **follow up a verbal notice of intended prosecution with a written notice of intended prosecution**.

Exam Trip Up

- Where jurisdiction falls between two counties a court in either county could hear the case - Kennet *DC v Young* [1999] RTR 235).

- For example - a driver committing an offence in Somerset, returns home to Dorset and fails to give their details to the officer as required.

D - Service Of A Notice Of Intended Prosecution – Section 1 Road Traffic Offenders Act 1988

A **notice** may be **served** by either:		
Option 1	**Option 2**	**Option 3**
Delivering it to them.	By **addressing** it to them and **leaving** it at their **last known place of address.**	By **sending** it to their **last known address** via either: ■ Registered post; ■ Recorded delivery; ■ First class post.

Exam Trip Up

If **option 3** is used – service will be **deemed** even when the notice is **<u>either:</u>**	
Not received.	Returned as undelivered.

Exam Trip Up - Service Upon Others On The Persons Behalf

- The case of *Hosier v Goodall* [1962] 1 All ER 30, established that it will be sufficient to serve a notice of intended prosecution **personally** on a:
  - ☐ **Partner;** or
  - ☐ **Spouse.**

Exam Trip Up – Service Despite Awareness Of Absence

- The case of *Phipps v McCormick* [1972] Crim LR 540, established that where a person is on **holiday or in hospital - service at their last known address will suffice** even if the police are aware the person was absent.

Exam Trip Up – Persons With No Fixed Abode

- If neither the defendant nor the registered keeper of the vehicle have any fixed abode - it is necessary to attempt to effect personal service.
- If it is not possible to effect personal service in such circumstances – service is dispensed with.

Exam Trip Up – Driver Has Contributed To Failure To Serve

- Section 24 of the Road Traffic Offenders Act 1988 states that if the defendant contributes to the failure to serve the NIP, then that failure will not be a bar to conviction.
- For example if a driver has failed to inform the DVLA of his change of address for several months, they have contributed to the failure for the NIP to be served.

Road Policing
Subject 10: Fixed Penalty System - Sergeants Syllabus Only

A - Definition Of A Fixed Penalty - Section 52 Road Traffic Offenders Act 1988

- A fixed penalty means:
  - A **notice;**
  - Offering the **opportunity** to **discharge** any **liability** for the **conviction** of an **offence** to which the notice relates;
  - By **payment** of a **fixed penalty.**

B – Fixed Penalty Procedure

The system envisages **two situations**:	
Driver Present	**Driver Absent**
Where the **driver** is **present.**	■ Where the driver is **absent**; *and* ■ There is a **statutory vehicle** to which the **notice** can be **attached.**

Issuing Fixed Penalties When The Driver Is Present

When May A Fixed Penalty Be Issued? - Section 54(1) Road Traffic Offenders Act 1988

A **constable** in **uniform**	A **vehicle examiner** who **produces** their **authority**
...may issue a fixed penalty if they have reason to **believe** that a person **either**:	
Is committing	**Has committed**
...a **fixed penalty offence.**	

Exam Trip Up

- Section 51 (2) of the Road Traffic Offenders Act 1988 specifies that a person may be issued only with a fixed penalty notice if the offence relates to the 'use' of the vehicle on a road.
- The system does not apply to those who 'cause' or 'permit' the use of a vehicle on a road while an offence is being committed.

Prerequisites To Be Satisfied Before The Fixed Penalty Is Issued - Section 54(3) Road Traffic Offenders Act 1988

The **constable** or **vehicle examiner** can only issue the fixed penalty if **all** of the following criteria are satisfied:		
Step 1	**Step 2**	**Step 3**
The person **produces for inspection** by the constable or vehicle examiner their: ■ **Licence;** ***and*** ■ **Its counterpart**;	The constable or vehicle examiner is satisfied, on inspection, that the person would **not be liable to disqualification.**	The person **surrenders** their: ■ **Licence;** ***and*** ■ **Its counterpart.**
If the person **cannot satisfy all of the criteria** - the constable or vehicle examiner may issue a **notice** requiring them to **surrender** their **licence** and its **counterpart** within **7 days.**		

Production Of A Notice, Licence And Its Counterpart To A Police Station - Section 54(5) Road Traffic Offenders Act 1988

What Must Be Produced?

Document 1	Document 2	Document 3
The **notice.**	Their **licence.**	Its **counterpart.**

How Must The Items Be Produced?

- The production provisions **differ** depending on whether the notice was issued by a constable or a vehicle examiner.

Factor	Notice Issued By A Constable	Notice Issued By A Vehicle Examiner
Method Of Production?	In person	By post or In person
Time Frame?	7 days	14 days
Location To Produce?	Police station chosen by the driver.	To the Secretary of state at the place specified in the notice.

Action To Be Taken Following A Production - Section 54(5) Road Traffic Offenders Act 1988

The constable or authorised person **must issue a fixed penalty** if the person <u>**both**</u>:	
Criteria 1	**Criteria 2**
Is **not subject to a disqualification** if convicted.	**Surrenders their licence.**

Exam Trip Up

- The **constable** must be **in uniform** to issue a fixed penalty.

Exam Trip Up

- If the person surrenders their licence at a police station, they can only be given a fixed penalty if it **does not take them to 12 points or above.**
- Section 55 (3) of the Road Traffic Act 1988 states that if the person has not paid a fixed penalty, or given notice requesting a court hearing by the end of the enforcement period, the police can register a sum equal to 1.5 times the amount of the penalty for enforcement against that person.
- There is nothing within the Act which stipulates that the police cannot request that the fine be increased for a 'parking offence' or other minor FPN matter.

Exam Trip Up

If the **offence** is **endorsable -** the fixed penalty can only be given if **both**:	
Criteria 1	**Criteria 2**
The person **surrenders** their **licence.**	The fixed penalty does **not take them to 12 points or more.**

Exam Trip Up – Statutory Declaration

- If a person receives a notice stating that a fixed penalty notice (FPN) has not been paid, he may **serve** a **statutory declaration** to the court, to the effect either:
    - That he was **not the person who was given the FPN**; or
    - That he has **given a notice requesting a court hearing**.
- In either case, the statutory notice must be made and served within 21 days of receiving the notice from the Clerk.

Exam Trip Up – Foreign and Unlicensed Drivers

- Section 54 of the Road Traffic Offenders Act 1988 has been amended to facilitate the endorsement of a drivers record held at the DVLA for unlicensed and foreign drivers.

Procedure When The Driver Is Not Present - Section 62(1) Road Traffic Offenders Act 1988

- If a **constable** has reason to **believe** that a **fixed penalty offence** either:
    - **Is being committed**; or
    - **Has been committed;**
- By a **stationary vehicle;**
- The **constable** may **affix** a **fixed penalty notice** to the **vehicle;**
- **Unless** the offence involves an **obligatory endorsement** (basically means points on your licence).

Exam Trip Up

- The **constable** need not be **in uniform** to issue the fixed penalty.

C – The Offences

Removing Or Interfering With Fixed Penalty Notice On Vehicle

Section 62(2) Road Traffic Offenders Act 1988
Summary Only Offence
Penalty In The Magistrates Court – Fine Only

A person is guilty of an offence if they **either**:		
Remove	**Interfere** with	
...any **notice fixed** to a **vehicle - unless** they do so with the **authority** of **either** the:		
Driver.	**Person in charge** of the vehicle.	**Person liable** for the fixed penalty.

Making False Statements In Relation To A Notice To An Owner

Section 67 Road Traffic Offenders Act 1988
Summary Only Offence
Penalty In The Magistrates Court – Fine Only

A person commits an offence if in **response** to a **notice** to the owner they **either:**	
Knowingly	**Recklessly**
...provide a **statement** which is **false** in a material particular.	

D - Conditional Offers – Section 75 Road Traffic Offenders Act 1988

Purpose Of A Conditional Offer

- The advent of **automatic devices for detecting speeding offences** precipitated the need to be able to issue a ticket in a way previously unavailable - namely by sending a **notice** to the alleged offender on **behalf** of the **Chief Constable.**

Contents Of A Conditional Offer - Section 75(1), (6), (7) & (8) Road Traffic Offenders Act 1988

The **notice** must:		
Fact 1	**Fact 2**	**Fact 3**
Outline the **offence** alleged	State the **amount** of the **fixed penalty**	State that **no proceedings** can take place for **28 days following** the date the **offer** was issued
...and indicate that if all of the following **conditions** are fulfilled any **liability to conviction** shall be **discharged:**		
Condition 1	**Condition 2**	**Condition 3**
Within 28 days the offender makes **payment** for the **fixed penalty** to the **fixed penalty clerk.**	Where there is an **obligatory endorsement**, at the **same time** the offender **delivers** their **licence** and **counterpart** to that clerk.	The **clerk** is **satisfied** that if convicted, the offender would **not be liable to disqualification.**

An Ineligible Person Has Tried To Accept A Conditional Offer - Section 76(4) Road Traffic Offenders Act 1988

In circumstances whereby both:	
a person is **sent a conditional offer of a fixed penalty notice** (FPN)...	....and that person is **liable for disqualification**
...then both:	
The payment along with the licence will be returned to the defendant...	...and the **police** will be **notified** thereby giving the police the opportunity to proceed by way of **summons.**

Immediate Financial Impositions

- The Road Traffic Offenders Act 1988, SS.90A-F empowers **police officers** or **vehicle examiners** to impose **immediate financial deposits** on any person who is committing an offence relating to a motor vehicle as may be specified in an order made by the Secretary of State.

- A **Vehicle Examiner** must **produce their authority** to do so and the **police officer** must be **in uniform**.

- Section 90D enables **police officers** or **vehicle examiners** to **prohibit** the **vehicle** from being **moved** if the **deposit is not paid immediately,** though the **vehicle may be moved to another specified place by written direction.**